THE INNOVATIONS

OF THE

ROMAN CHURCH

**BASED ON THE REPLY OF THE GREAT CHURCH
OF CONSTANTINOPLE TO THE
ENCYCLICAL ISSUED BY POPE LEO XIII IN 1894
CONCERNING THE UNION OF THE CHURCHES**

By
APOSTOLOS   MAKRAKIS
(1831 – 1905)

Published by the
ORTHODOX CHRISTIAN EDUCATIONAL SOCIETY
Chicago, Illinois

PRINTED IN
ATHENS, GREECE
First Edition, 1948
Second Edition, 1966

PREFACE

The main text of the present work has been taken from pages of the weekly religious periodical entitled "Logos", edited by A. Makrakis, the great expounder of Orthodoxy, and includes not only the most important paragraphs of the "Reply of the Great Church of Constantinople to the Encyclical of Pope Leo XIII" respecting reunion of the churches, but also much pertinent matter bearing upon the questions involved and drawn either from the foregoing periodical or from the Holy Scriptures themselves. Quotations of Apostolic and of Synodical Canons are from the well-known book of the Orthodox Church called the "Pedalion," a compilation of the canons of the Seven Ecumenical Councils.

The object of this book is to enlighten the reader concerning truths which have remained hidden and unknown to the public in regard to Papal Primacy and the innovations introduced by the Papal Church, while at the same time reminding him of the duties and obligations of Orthodox Christians in support of the truth for their own interest and spiritual welfare.

THE EDITORS

PREFACE

THE INNOVATIONS OF THE ROMAN CHURCH

The reply of the Church of Constantinople to the Encyclical of the Pope concerning union of the Churches was published in the patriarchical **Truth.** Therein are expressed, on the one hand, the sorrow of the Great Church at the separation, and, on the other, the desire for union of the Eastern and Western Churches, which have been separated for ten centuries, in the single canon of faith, without which no desirable union of the Churches is possible.

The reply of the Great Church of Constantinople assumes as the basis of right faith the doctrine of the New Testament and of the seven holy Ecumenical Synods, which was common to both Churches during the first eight centuries of Christianity. It is on this basis, it says, that the papacy must be judged and the innovations critically discussed which were adopted in the West before and after the separation. It points out the papal innovations, and discusses each in accordance with the criterion of the doctrine of the Scriptures and seven Ecumenical Synods:

1) It characterizes as the first innovation the doctrine that the Holy Spirit proceeds also from the Son *(Filioque)*.

2) As the second it cites the substitution of affusion (sprinkling) for baptism by trine immersion.

3) It denounces as the third innovation the substitution of **unleavened** wafers for **the leavened bread** thitherto in use in the sacrament of the Eucharist—an innovation dating from the eleventh century.

4) As the fourth it brings up the doctrine that the precious gifts are sanctified with the enunciation of the Lord's words, "Take, eat," etc. and "Drink ye of it all," etc., whereas the Eastern Church holds that the sanctification occurs at the prayer for the invocation of the Holy Spirit through the blessing of the priest.

5) The fifth innovation to be considered is the Western Church's exclusion of the laity from partaking of the precious blood of the Savior.

6) As the sixth innovation it censures the doctrine concerning a purgatory fire, that concerning superabundance of the saints' virtues and their distribution to those in need of them, and that concerning full retribution of the righteous before the common resurrection and judgment take place.

7) As the seventh it points out the dogma concerning the immaculate conception of the Theotokos (Virgin Mary) decreed seventy five years ago by the Synod held at the Vatican.

8) Lastly, it discusses papal **primacy,** and proves by reference to the Fathers and the Canons of the Ecumenical Synods that the Pope was never considered the supreme authority and infallible head of the Church, but only the first bishop in respect of rank, as first among **equals,** privileges of honor having been accorded to him because he was the bishop of the capital city of the Empire; but similar honorary privileges were later accorded to the bishop of Constantinople also, because Constantinople had become the new seat of the Roman Empire.

Finally, in her reply to the Pope's Encyclical concerning union of the two Churches, the Great Church urges Orthodox Christians to hold firmly to the faith of their Fathers, and dissenters to unite with the ancient Church by repudiating the insinuated innovations and adopting the single canon of faith of the ancient Church.

To the Papal Church's demands concerning union the Orthodox Church has from the beginning retorted with **the single canon of faith** embodied in the doctrine of the Holy Scriptures and the seven Ecumenical Synods, and has discussed Western innovations with circumspection. But the **infallible** Pope refuses to listen to reason, being unable to understand that he is laboring in vain and that he only makes himself ridiculous by laying claim to infallibility. He persists in imagining himself to be the infallible head of the Church and insists that all persons submit to him on pain of eternal punishment.

Our Church, however, being confident that her head is Jesus Christ and that she is enlightened by the Holy Spirit, remains faithful to the ancient traditions and refutes the sophisms of papal arrogance with proofs showing the faultiness of the doctrines advocated by him who lays claim to infallible inspiration but is unable to understand that he is laboring in vain and only kicking against the goads (*)

(*) The above is quoted from the journal "Logos" of Athens, Greece, issue number 1129, of the year 1895. A lengthy reply to the Pope's Encyclical was also given by Basil, the then Metropolitan Bishop of Smyrna in an encyclical of his numbered 1113.

THE HEAD AND FOUNDATION OF THE CHURCH

The head of the Church of Christ, says Paul the Apostle of the heathen, is Christ: "...the God of our Lord Jesus Christ, the Father of glory,... when he raised him from the dead, and set him at his right hand in the heavenly realm, far above every principality, and authority, and power, and dominion, and every name that is named, not only in this world, but also in that which is to come; and put all things in subjection under his feet, and gave him to be head over all things to the church, which is his body, the complement of him who is filled all in all." (*Eph.* 1.23). And again: "who is the head, even Christ." (*Eph.* 4.16). And elsewhere: "And he is the head of the body, the church, who is the beginning, the firstborn from the dead, that in all things he may enjoy preeminence." (*Col.* 1.18). And again: "Beware lest anyone be making spoil of you through philosophy and vain deceit, after the tradition of men, after the elements of the world, and not after Christ; for in him dwelleth all the complement of the Deity bodily, and in him ye are filled, who is the head of every principality and authority." (*Col.* 2.8-10).

Contrariwise, however, the Popes of the Roman Church distinguish a visible and an invisible head. Accordingly, they make themselves the visible head, and Christ the invisible head; and they assert that the Pope who happens to be in office should rule the Church of Christ on earth in His name. But who ever gave them such authority? The great dragon, as we shall see farther on.

But the head of the Church is Christ, and none other but Christ, whom the Father twice recommended to the Church by the voice speaking out of heaven as well as out of the cloud—out of heaven, when Jesus was being baptized by John in the Jordan, by saying: "This is my beloved Son, of whom I approve." (*Matt.* 3.17; *Mark* 1.11; *Luke* 3.22); and out of the bright cloud, when Jesus was transfigured on Mount Tabor in the presence of His three outstanding disciples, Peter, James, and John, the same voice was again heard to say: "This is my beloved Son, of whom I approve; hear ye him." (*Matt.* 17.5). In other words: "O Jews and all other persons, up till now ye have extolled me as your God and your Lord; and rightly, too, for so I am. But henceforth I shall be pleased and wish to have you obey my beloved Son, Jesus Christ."

It is to be noted, too, that those who obey the voice of the heavenly Father and submit to the Son, have also the Father; whereas those who deny the Son have neither the Father, as is written: "Whoever denieth the Son, the same hath not the Father either." (1 *John* 2.23). And those who recognize another head, the Pope, instead of the Son, not only disregard the voice of the Father, but even oppose His wishes. Woe to them according to what is written: "It is a fearful thing to fall into the hands of the living God." (*Heb.* 10.31).

It is further to be noted that through the incarnation of the Son of God the Holy Trinity—Father, Son ,and Holy Spirit—was made known: the Father, by the word of mouth spoken out of heaven and that uttered out of the bright cloud; the Son, by His being baptized and transfigured; the Holy Spirit by His assuming the shape of a dove and of a bright cloud. Those, therefore, who persist in a belief in only one God (monotheists)—Jews and Mohammedans, Students of the Bible or Jehovah Witnesses, and all others who deny the Son and the Holy Spirit—have neither the Father; they remain implacable enemies of Christ and of Christianity unless and until they change their mind are baptized in the name of the Holy Trinity.

The Foundation : "For other foundation can no one lay than which has been laid, which is Jesus Christ." (1 *Cor.* 3.11). "And are built upon the foundation of the apostles and prophets, Jesus Christ himself being the chief cornerstone." (*Eph.* 2.20). "Behold, I lay in Zion a chief cornerstone, elect, precious; and that believeth on him shall not be put to shame." (*Is.* 28.16). Christ, therefore, is not only the head of the Church, but also its infallible foundation. "And I say also unto thee, that thou art Peter, and upon this rock I will build my church; and the gates of Hades shall not prevail against it." (*Matt.* 16.18).

The Pope, not content with the title of Pontifex of Rome, waxing envious of the Caesars, or Emperors, of Rome who preceded him, boastingly asserts that while Christ is the invisible head of the Church, the Pope is the visible head. In thus usurping the position of head of the Church, he necessarily also usurps that of its declared foundation stone, since the Pope has built in the name of Jesus a church of his own and to his own liking and desire. But against him will be fulfilled that which is written: "The stone which the builders rejected is become the head of the corner. Whosoever shall fall upon that stone shall be broken to pieces, but on whomsoever it shall fall, it will scatter him as dust." (Luke 20.17). That very same stone will soon scatter all nations as dust, because of the scribes and Pharisees and the infallible Popes of Rome.

THE TRUE REPRESENTATIVE OF CHRIST ON EARTH

After the Ascension of Christ who was seated at the right hand of the Father, the primacy in His Church was taken over by the Holy Spirit which St. Paul calls the Lord, saying: "Now the Lord is the Spirit". (2 *Cor.* 3.17). Christ did not deliver the primacy in His Church to any of the Apostles, but only to the Holy Spirit which descended in the form of fiery tongues upon all the Apostles during Holy Pentecost, as is written: "These things have I spoken unto you ,being yet present with you. But the Comforter, who is the Holy Spirit and whom the Father will send in my name, shall teach you all things, and bring all things to your remembrance whatsoever I have said unto you." (*John* 14.25-26). "I have yet many things to say unto you, but ye cannot bear them now. Howbeit, when he, the Spirit of Truth, is come, he will guide you into all truth: for he will not speak from himself; but whatsoever he shall hear, that will he speak, and he will declare unto you the things that are to come." (*John* 16.12). "I will not leave you orphans; I will come to you." (*John* 14.18).

From the above-quoted words of Jesus the absolute truth and faith is to be gathered that the Holy Spirit has the primacy and infallibility in the Church and guides it into all the truth, just as he guided the holy Apostles at Pentecost and thereafter St. Paul and the other Apostles and holy Fathers and the Martyrs who were slaughtered while upholding the name of the Lord Jesus Christ.

PRIMACY AND INFALLIBILITY

The holy Apostles being gathered together at a synod and engaged in a discussion of the question of circumcision, Apostle Peter spoke first and then James, and finally they wrote to the Christians, among other things, the following: "For it seemed good to the Holy Spirit, and to us, to lay upon you no greater burden than these necessary things: ..." (*Acts* 15.28), whence it is plain that Apostle Peter had no primacy, but that he attributed the primacy to the Holy Spirit; "for it seemed good to the Holy Spirit, and to us," he says, and not to Peter alone. "And the Spirit bade me (Peter) go with them, nothing doubting." (*Acts* 11.12). Where is

Peter's primacy? In the Spirit. "As they ministered to the Lord, and fasted, the Holy Spirit said, Separate me Barnabas and Paul for the work whereunto I have called them." (*Acts* 13.2). "...having been forbidden by the Holy Spirit to preach the word in Asia, on coming to Mysia, they essayed to go to Bythynia; but the Spirit suffered them not." (*Acts* 16.6-7). "Paul was constrained by the Spirit" (*Acts* 18.5). "And now, behold, bound in the Spirit I go to Jerusalem... Take heed therefore, unto yourselves, and to all the flock, wherein the Holy Spirit hath made you bishops to shepherd the Church of God, which he hath purchased with his own blood". (*Acts* 20.22 and 28).

The primacy and dominion of the Holy Spirit over the Church after the Ascension of Jesus Christ is established also by these above-cited passages from the Acts of the Apostles. Those, therefore, who lay claim to primacy and infallibility in the Church of Christ are totally deluded.

THE ALLEGED PRIMACY
AND INFALLIBILITY OF THE POPES

In the year of our Lord 829 the Pope forged a letter from some fictitious monk called Isidore, which he falsely attributed to St. Isidore. And by means of these fictitious Isidorian decretals he was proclaimed supreme ruler of the Church by divine right and invested with the right to judge all persons without being liable to be judged himself by anyone else. In the name of the false principle which the Popes proclaimed as a divine principle, the Popes committed all sorts of illicit and base acts with which the history of the Middle Ages abounds.

"And I beheld another beast coming up out of the earth; and he had two horns (of authority), like a lamb, and he spoke as a dragon." (*Rev.* 13.11). The Holy Spirit prophesied through the Revelation of the beloved disciple John the Divine that after the appearance of the first beast, or Mohammed the Antichrist (who made his first appearance A.D. 605), another beast would make his appearance and would exercise two authorities, and would appear outwardly like a lamb, but inwardly like a dragon.

According to this express declaration of the Holy Spirit, the Pope is the beast coming up out of the earth, which has two horns like a lamb and speaks like a dragon. For outwardly the Pope does indeed appear to exercise authority and rule in the name of Christ and the Gospel, but inwardly he is inspired by the Devil himself, the dragon, and through him the Devil speaks and deceives those who dwell upon the earth, and through him he rules religiously and politically among his followers. The Pope, then, according to the declaration of the Holy Spirit, is the pseudo-Christ who with his hypocrisy succeeded in misleading the ignorant peoples of the West during the Middle Ages into believing that he was the representative of Christ on the earth and the holder of the keys to Paradise and could by collecting money for indulgences and grant anybody admission to Paradise.

The ignorant peoples of the West believed this charlatanial myth, on the basis of which the religious and political authority of the Pope was created, and thus was consolidated his illegal authority, to which are due the many ills which resulted and continue to result in Europe and other parts of the world following his appearance,—such as Protestantism, materialism, the atheism of Voltaire and the Encyclopedists in France, and the wars between Christians and Christians.

In the Roman Church, proudly but falsely calling itself Catholic, we find it firmly established as a fundamental and saving dogma that the Pope who happens to be in office at any time is Christ's representative and St. Peter's successor, and consequently the chief and highest of all bishops and one to whom all owe blind obedience and submission. Boniface, Pope of Rome during the thirteenth century, wrote a letter to King Philip of France in which he ended by saying: "We state and declare the belief that every human creature is subject to the Pope of Rome is necessary for future bliss." On the insignia of Pope Pius IV is to be read the following confession: "I confess the Holy, Catholic, Roman, and Apostolic Church to be the mother and mistress of all other churches; and I promise true submission to the bishop of Rome, successor of St. Peter, chief of the Apostles, and representative of Jesus Christ."

This, furthermore, is an official dogma decreed by the Council of Trent, which was held by the Papists in the sixteenth century to settle the general policy, principles, and dogmas of the Roman Church, and which invested Papal primacy with divine validity. One of the consequences of this dogma of Papal primacy has been the notorious dogma of Papal Infallibility, and, by implication, that of Papal impeccability, since he who is infallible can commit no sin. Being infallible and impeccable, the Pope has no need of any law, for he holds direct communion with the Holy Spirit, and has no need of advisers or of recourse to the Holy Scriptures, and, being infallible and equal to God and to Christ, he is in a position to lay down the law to the Church. Consequently, his words, and, by implication, his deeds, are the law of the Papists and of the whole Papal Church.

But this false dogma of infallibility and impeccability has been proved fallacious, erroneous, and Satanical by its consequences, by history, by the fact that the Popes themselves disagree and quarrel about the dogmas of faith with other Popes,—their colleagues and predecessors—and by the fact that some of the Popes have even become heretics—as examples of such Popes we may mention that Pope Honorius adhered to the heresy of the Monothelites and was condemned as a heretic by the Sixth Ecumenical Council; Hadrian II, Pope of Rome, was excommunicated as a heretic for the same heresy by Leo II, Pope of Rome, who, in turn, became guilty of heresy and was condemned as such.

A second proof is the fact that many of the Popes, especially after the Schism, were excedingly wanton and lustful, murderers, debauchers, conspirators, forgers—one of them forged the pseudo-Isidorian tenets after the schism in order to lay a foundation and support for Papal Primacy with a view to undermining the true Church and combating its authority. In fact, it is recorded in history that some of the Popes supposted a number of women and even maintained whole sultanic harems; some of the Popes were even elevated to the Papal throne and governed by the lewdest sort of women. Many were simoniacs who trafficked in the sacred orders, in consequence whereof they became the creators of indulgences by which they sold Paradise for money to the ignorant people who could afford to buy them. In addition to all this, they were persecutors of education and of the Holy Scriptures, and extinguishers of the light who wished to keep the rest of humanity in ignorance and illiteracy so that they might exact from it blind obedience and in the name of infallibility and exemption from censure do whatever they might please. Where, then, is the evidence for the Popes' Infallibility and impeccability. Only in their heads. In the deeds of their lives is to be seen everything to the contrary thereof.*

THE MARK OF THE BEAST
THAT SPEAKS LIKE A DRAGON

"And I beheld another beast coming up out of the earth; and he had two horns, like a lamb, and he spoke as a dragon. And he causeth all, both small and great, rich and poor, free and bond, to receive a mark upon their right hand or upon their foreheads, and that no one may buy or sell, save he that hath the mark, or the name of the beast, or the number of his name. Here is wisdom. Let him that hath understanding count the number of the beast; for it is the number of a man, and his number is Six Hundred and sixty-six." (*Rev.* 13.11 and 16-18).

Dragon : "Dragon" is another name for the Devil, who entered the Serpent and misinterpreted the divine law to Eve, and who killed man by fraud and deceit, having induced him to violate the divine law. (*Rom.* 5.12-21; 7.8-26).

"Spoke as a dragon" means that he rivalled the dragon in mendacity, hypocrisy, deceit, and misinterpretation of the divine law. The Pope pretends to be the representative of Christ, but has perverted the divine law to his own perdition and that of his followers.

"Coming up out of the earth": By "earth" is meant the civilized world, and particularly the land of Italy, just as "sea" means the barbarian peoples of the first beast, or the Arabs. The meaning of "two horns, like a lamb" and of "beast" has already been explained, on page 4.

"A mark upon their right hand or upon their foreheads" means the sign of the cross as made by Roman Catholics; for they do not make it by uniting the three fingers to signify the dogma of the Holy Trinity, as do we Orthodox Christians, but, spreading apart all five fingers, they place them upon their foreheads, and

---

(*)For a detailed account of the crimes committed by the Popes, see **History of Romanism** by Rev. John Bowling, A.M., 3rd ed., N. Y. 1845; also **The Woman Who Was Pope,** a biography of Pope Joan (A.D. 853-5), by Clement Wood, N.Y. 1931, William Fate, Inc. If neither of these illuminating works in accessible, the reader is advised to consult Draper's **Intellectual History of Europe** and the works of Joseph McCabe, himself a former Roman Catholic and for years a professor of philosophy in the Roman Catholic Church.

dip them in water (the so-called holy water of the Pope) as they enter the church. This is the mark which the beast conferred upon his followers to distinguish them from other Christians. According to the Papists themselves, the five fingers denote the Holy Trinity, the Virgin Mary, and the Pope.

"The name of the beast": We can tell the name of the beast, it says, or his image, from the number of his name, which is Six Hundred and Sixty-six, by counting the letters representing the number. The Greek letters taken numerically denote in the case of X600, of S60, and of C6, totaling 666. What name corresponds to this number? The name **Latin** as spelled in Greek! A30, A1, T300, E5, I10, N50, 070, S200, which added together make a total of 666. This is the "mark" of the beast and that of his followers—the name (of the beast), Latin (Papist or Roman Catholic), or the number of the beast.

"I marvel," says the chosen vessel, "that you have so soon been withdrawing from him who called you into the grace of Christ, unto another gospel, which is not another except that there are some who are disturbing you and who would pervert the gospel of Christ. But though we, or an angel from heaven, should preach any gospel to you other than that which we have preached to you, let him be anathema. As we said before, so say I now again, if anyone preach any other gospel unto you than that which ye have received, let him be anathema." (*Gal.* 1.6-8).

Of the five Patriarchs of the Church, that of Rome as the bishop of the capital of the vast Roman Empire and having a very large territory under his spiritual jurisdiction was allowed "the primacy of honor" as a first among equals. But the Popes sought to recover the real primacy and supremacy formerly enjoyed by the antichristian idolatrous Caesars, or emperors, of ancient

---

NOTE.—The name Latin was written in Greek with **EI**, as were many other words usually spelled with **I** alone; this spelling was especially common in the case of the ending **-INOE**, in which the **I** is long, due to aphaeresis of the **E**. Irenaeus, bishop of Lyons, an ancient Apostolic Father who flourished about A.D. 183, writes the names Titan, Latin, etc. with **EI** instead of **I** (Book V,30). A great number of examples of **EI** instead of **I** long occur in Greek inscriptions even before Christ, as, for instance, KALLINEIKOY (Inscr. 1053), instead of KALLINIKOY. Quintilian (1,7.75), too, and other Roman scholars acquainted with the Greek language assert that long **I** was frequently written **EI**. For other instances see G. Meyer's **Griechische Grammatic**, 3te Aufl., Leipzig, 1897, or E.A. Sophocles' **Greek Lexicon of the Roman Byzantine Periods** (from B.C. 146 to A.D. 1100), Cambridge, Mass., Harvard University Press, 1941, under the Diagraph **EI**.

Rome, which was abolished by Constantine the Great. They based their claim upon their alleged Apostolical succession from St. Peter the Apostle as the alleged first bishop of Rome, to whom the Lord allegedly granted the primacy in the Church when He said to Peter: "Thou art Peter, and upon this rock I will build my Church; and the gates of Hell shall not prevail against it." (*Matt.* 16.18). But by the word "rock" the Lord meant Peter's confession, "Thou art the Christ, the Son of the living God." The Popes, however, take the word "rock" to mean Peter, to whom, by consequence, they assert, passed the primacy in the Church; which is like arguing that oranges are gold-colored because the noun **or** means gold.

The Popes began introducing innovations and seeking the primacy about the beginning of the ninth century, but were courageously repulsed by great Photios, the patriarch of Constantinople, who, through a synod held in the year 879, composed of 383 bishops, opposed the claims of the Popes, and the decision of the synod was signed by Paul and Eugene, the representatives of Pope John VIII. But after the death of Photios, the Popes intensified their claims to the primacy, thought their endeavors were in vain; for when a delegation under Cardinal Humbert arrived in Constantinople and claimed the primacy, all relations with them were severed. Seeing that he could accomplish nothing on this occasion, the enraged cardinal entered the cathedral of St. Sophia on the 16th day of July, A.D. 1054, during the celebration of divine Liturgy, therein, and laid upon the Holy Table an excommunication of the Patriarch and of the entire Eastern Church, after which he and his party departed in haste from Constantinople.

Michael, however, the Patriarch, convoked a numerous synod on July 20th of the same year, in which the Pope and all those who had blasphemed against Orthodoxy were excommunicated. Thenceforth all relations between the Orthodox and the Roman Catholic Church were severed, which condition still remains, with the Pope laying claim to primacy and infallibility.

Schism: the term **schism** and **shismatics** are applied to those who refuse to submit to the Synods of the Ecumenical Patriarch, but persist in the same dogma of Orthodoxy; as, e.g., the schism of the Bulgarian Orthodox Church. But as between Orthodoxy and the Papal Church there is no schism, but a heresy, because the Popes innovated dogmas contrary to the principles of Orthodoxy. Nevertheless, because the notion of separation is attached to this

2

term by common usage, it still remains in use in this sense among some Orthodox Christians, and, unfortunately, even among the clergy, to the great detriment of Orthodoxy and the Orthodox Church.

Nowhere in Ecclesiastical History is there any mention of St. Peter's having at any time been a bishop of Rome, or of any other church, for that matter. Nor does St. Paul, in writing his epistles from Rome, allude to anything of the kind, although, if St. Peter had really been a bishop of Rome, it seems inevitable that his name would have been mentioned by St. Paul, particularly in his second epistle to Timothy, where Linus, who is known to have been a bishop of Rome, is mentioned (2 *Tim.* 4.21). Morover, in his epistle to the Romans, writing from Corinth, St. Paul sent greetings to his brethren in Rome, of whom he mentions many by name (*Rom.*, ch. 16), but does not refer to St. Peter at all, whose name he could not have omitted had St. Peter been bishop of Rome in point of fact. Peter the Apostle did, however, found the church of Antioch in Caesaria (*Acts*, ch. 10). This being so, we ought to recognize the Patriarch of Antioch as the real successor to St. Peter, and not the Pope of Rome, St. Peter is said to have suffered martyrdom in Rome, as did also St. Paul, during the reign of Nero, about A.D. 68-69.

The Lord Himself appointed the first bishop of Christ's Church, choosing as such James the brother of God, whom He made bishop of Jerusalem, and from whom we have inherited the Holy Liturgy, which was in use up to the time of Basil the Great, who shortened it somewhat. When James suffered martyrdom, he was succeeded by his brother Simeon. The first bishop of Rome was Linus, who held office during the reign of Emperor Titus; the second was Anecletus, and the third, Clement. (Eusebius, *Ecc. Hist.* pp. 77-81).

It is to these Satanical claims to primacy and infallibility of the Popes that all the innovations of the Roman Catholic Church are due, as well as their claim to temporal authority, of which they have been shorn gradually until only a vestige of it remains; and it is to be hoped and expected that they will soon be shorn of their religious authority likewise through the power of the precious and life-giving Cross, according to prophecy. Amen.

THE FIRST INNOVATION: FILIOQUE

The first innovation (or heresy) was the addition to the eighth article of the Symbol of Faith (or Creed) of the Latin words **"filioque,"** meaning "and from the Son," and signifying that the Holy Spirit proceeds from the Father and from the Son, contrary to the words of our Lord, who said: "But when the Comforter cometh, whom I will send unto you from the Father, the Spirit of Truth, who proceedeth from the Father, he shall bear witness of me." (John 15.26). The addition "and from the Son" bisects the hypostasis of the Holy Spirit, cutting it in two, so to speak, and makes the Son a father—an allegation which is nothing short of blasphemous and heretical.

The Second Ecumenical Synod, which supplemented the Creed of the First, defined that no one has the right to add anything to or to substract anything from the Symbol of Faith, or Creed, as established by it. The minutes of both these Synods were attested and signed by the representatives of the Popes then holding office. The addition of **"filioque"** is a blasphemy against the Holy Spirit, and the source of it is the Devil, also called the Dragon; and, according to the words of the Lord, it will be forgiven "neither in this world nor in the world to come."

"Proceedeth" signifies the manner of generation, and not the act of sending nor the fact of being sent. The Son is begotten only by the Father; but the Spirit, too, proceedeth only from the Father, or, as is more to the point and closer to the meaning of the Greek word in question, is **yielded** only by the Father: two branches from the same root, brothers, as it were; effects of the causeless, initial, and absolute cause; timeless, eternal, inalterable, everlasting, because their being is derived hypostatically from the timeless, eternal, inalterable, and everlasting Father; being simultaneously, and not alternatingly, at the same time the Father, at the same time the Son, and together and at the same time the Spirit. Mind, Speech, and Spirit—or, **Nous, logos,** and **Pneuma;** the first Mind (Father) begets (generates) the Speech or Word (Logos) and yields (prolates) the Spirit to the Logos and Son, and through Him to the Church. That is why the Lord Said: "whom the Father will send in my name." Jesus, as victor, legally acquired the right to send the Spirit to the Church, and the Father send the Spirit in His name.

The representative, therefore, of the militant Church of Christ on the earth is the Comforter, or Paraclete, a perfect God from the perfect God and Father, immortal and infallible. St. Peter and the other Apostles and Holy Fathers and teachers of the Church are faithful servants of the Holy Spirit, though sinful and mortal, yet the decisions of the many when convened and gathered together in one and the same place in Holy Spirit possess legal validity in the Church, but not the decisions of each singly, one by one. All pastors or teachers who oppose or defy the Canons of the Apostles and Ecumenical Synods or the text of the Holy Scriptures, err and build on sand. The Papal innovations and councils are invalid and illegal, because they oppose and defy the decisions of the Apostles and Ecumenical Synods and the text of the Holy Scriptures. "Let God be true, and every man a liar." (Rom. 3.4). The innovations, therefore, and decisions of the Pope, claiming primacy, must be combated until they disappear from the province of the Church. Let us hope that this may be speedily consummated.

Respecting the triune character of the Deity and the relations between the three persons of the Trinity, Christian theology teaches that God is essentially **one** and that He is the cause and Creator of all things, but that He exists in three coeternal persons; of whom the first person is the Father—Mind unbegotten, the second person is the Son—Logos eternally begotten of the Father Mind, and the third person is the Holy Spirit—Thought eternally yielded by only the Father Mind and revealed and sent in time to the world through the Son. Both the Son-Logos and the Spirit-Thought, however, are due to one and the same cause and eternal principle, the Father-Mind; and they are co-essential with the Principle from which the Son-Logos is begotten and the Spirit-Thought is yielded, or pre-lated (i.e., is caused and given forth), eternally. The terms **begat** and **yield** signify the manner of production and the relation of the Son-Logos and of the Spirit-Thought to the Father-Mind, by whom the one is begotten and the other yielded. But how are the terms **begotten** and **yielded** to be differentiated logically?

The first Being, the beginningless and unbegotten Mind, who, cognizing Himself through Himself eternally, produces, in cognizing Himself, the Idea of Himself, which, of course, is like Him and is His exact image and similitude, as well as the first Truth and pre-sentation of Him, being, in fact, an Idea of the first Mind, or of the first Being, equal to God, substantial (hypostatic), personal, posses-sing beinghood and entity. For if it were otherwise, it would conse-quently be merely an imaginary (fantastic) idea and imperfect; but a perfect Mind cognizing Himself imperfectly would not be a perfect Mind at all. It follows, then, that the perfect Mind educes out of Himself a single perfect Idea of Himself, and thus begets, or generates, one who is consubstantial with Him, that is to say, one of the same substance. And because the Idea of the perfect Mind perfectly presents and pictures the first Mind, it is consequently also the first Truth, inasmuch as truth is a true and exact picture and presentation of whatever is. The manner in which the Idea is produced by the Mind is called **begetting** or **generation,** for it is similar to the begetting of a son by a father. But the relation of the Spirit-Thought to the Mind is different from that of the Son-Logos being begotten by the Father-Mind.

The Spirit, as the cognitive power of the Mind—as Thought, that is to say—is yielded (prolated) by the Mind and out of the Mind as by and out of an eternal source, much in the same way as mother's milk is yielded by and out of the breasts, as water flows from a spring, as fruit is yielded by a tree, or wool by a sheep. It reposes in the Son-Logos as It is yielded by the Father-Mind. The expression and production of the Spirit-Thought by and out of the Father-Mind is called **yield,** or **procession,** because it is similar to the yielding of milk by a mother, the flowing of water from a spring, the growth of wool from a sheep, the production of fruit by a tree, and the emission and radiation of light by the sun. Thus the Spirit-Thought is yielded by and proceeds from the Father-Mind, a perfect being from a perfect being, equal to and co-essential with the Father-Mind, a perfect personality proceeding only from that Father-Mind but reposing, or resting, in the Son-Logos, and being emitted and sent forth through the Son-Logos to those cognitive essences who are capable of receiving the latter. In fine, **procession** denotes the perpetual, the eternal emanation, emission, effusion, production, while **transmission** denotes Its being sent and passed on by and through the Son-Logos. The two words, in bold type are not, of course, exact translations of the corresponding terms used in the original Greek, **ekporeusis** and **pompe** respectively, to which there are no equivalents in the English language nor in the Latin. That is why we have gone to such lengths in explaining just what they mean. Although the verbs **yield** and **grant** approach the true meaning of the Greek terms more closely than do the words **procession** and **transmission,** the use of them in this connection is attended with the inconvenience due to the lack of corresponding nouns distinguishable from the verbs and capable of being used in the same sense.

But the Roman Catholics confuse the transmission in time of the Spirit through the Son with the eternal procession thereof from the Father-Mind alone, wrongly assuming and holding that the Spirit's procession is due to two factors,, the Father-Mind and the Son-Logos, which is absurd, for it implies an imperfection in both the producing Mind and the proceeding Spirit. If the Mind does not yield a perfect Spirit, then the Mind is by consequence imperfect, and the Spirit, or Thought, imperfect as well. But a mind thinking imperfectly, and having an imperfect thought, is not a perfect mind. Consequently it is plain that the Spirit-Thought proceeds perfect out of the perfect Mind alone, though It reposes in the Son-Logos, through whom It is also sent forth to the world, being granted in time for enlightenment and knowledge. In God, therefore, there are three eternal and perfect beings, to-wit: 1) the Father-Mind; 2) the Son-Logos, His Idea; and 3) the Spirit, His Thought. Logos of God, Spirit of God, and God, the name of the essence of the perfect Being; Father, Logos, and Spirit—the names of the three co-eternal hypostases, or persons, of the one co-essential Deity. God the Father, or Mind; God the Son and Logos, or Idea; God the Spirit, or Throught—one triune God. The distinction between the three hypostases may be seen from the fact that the Father-Mind is an uncaused cause, whereas the Son-Logos and the Spirit-Thought are causates co-eternal with the cause, and therefore are products, the Son-Logos being begotten and the Spirit-Thought being yielded by Him out of whom It proceedeth. Such is the concept of the one and triune God according to the Orthodox dogma and the Orthodox theology; and such is the logical explanation of the fact that the Son-Logos is **begotten,** and of the fact that the Spirit-Thought is yielded, and not that it merely proceeds of Itself, and also of the fact that the Spirit is transmitted and sent through the Son-Logos. Such, indeed, is the relation by which the one and only true God, a Unity and a Trinity, can be conceived and understood just as He is lauded and glorified by our fathers and just as all Orthodox Christians believe and confess Him through the Creed, or Symbol of Faith. This relation becomes more clearly discernible by studying the following illustration.

When a man's soul clearly and distinctly knows itself and the things round and without—when it possesses knowledge of self and of God, it is called a **mind**. A soul that is naturally mindful and intelligent begets speech, or discourse presentative of its own ideas and judgments. Those who hear the discourse imbibe the thoughts of the soul talking ,without removing them either from the discourse or from the soul's mind. These thoughts are called **spirit**. Now, just as the soul's mind naturally begets discourse and expresses, or emits, through its discourse thought and spirit to thousands of other souls, so the first and perfect Mind naturally begets the first and perfect Logos* and at the same time yields the first and perfect Spirit, which is effused and transmitted from the Logos and by the Logos to other minds for their enlightenment and knowledge. And just as the mind, the discourse, and the spirit of the soul are distinct yet united, naturally correlated and inseparable as regards the relation of the son to the father, of the picture to the original, and of flowing water to the source from which it springs, so do the same unity and distinctness and reference and relation exist as between God the Mind, God the Logos (Discourse), and God the Spirit, who for this reason is lauded and glorified as one and triune—a Unit in a Trinity and a Trinity in a Unit—Father, Son ,and Holy Spirit, the co-essential (homoousian) and inseparable Trinity.

We recommend to Roman Catholics, Protestants, and Jews the **New Philosophy and Philosophical Sciences** as the clew to salvation from the moral labyrinth into which they have fallen as a result of their misconception of the Holy Trinity and by remaining in which they are bound to become a prey to the figurative Minotaurus (Devil). By studying that work they will come to see the scientific truth about the essence and nature of the Holy Trinity, of the true God, and of the relation subsisting between the three persons as a truth that can be proved. In consequence they will be converted to the true faith of Orthodoxy for the sake of their own personal salvation, for only the truth can save, by leading its followers to the true end of their predestination, whereas error always leads its followers to an erroneous end departing widely from their predestination and life goal.

(*) Discourse or Speech, respecting which see the detailed account in Apostolos Makrakis, **A New Philosophy and the Philosophical Sciences,** Book V, Philosophy, published in 1940 in English by Putnam's Sons, New York, N.Y.

THE SECOND INNOVATION: AFFUSION OR ASPERSION

The Lord said: "...baptizing them in the name of the Father, and of the Son, and of the Holy Spirit." (*Matt.* 28.19).

The second innovation (heresy) of the Pope is pouring or sprinkling water on the person to be baptized, for the word **baptism** means dipping, and never means pouring or sprinkling — as anyone versed in the Greek language knows. The Latins "infallibly" assert that sprinkling (affusion or aspersion) was introduced and substituted for baptizing (immersion) because of the physiological effect of water so as not to endanger the lives of infants; but this practice is in direct violation of the express command of Jesus Christ. Baptism is of God; sprinkling is of the man who has apostatized from God. "We ought to obey God rather than men." (*Acts* 5.9). "Let God be true, but every man a liar; as it is written. That thou mayest be justified in thy words and mayest prevail when thou are judged". (*Rom.* 3.4).

In a word: Baptism is of Christ, sprinkling is of Satan, the inventor of evils. Christ is true and is truth itself, whereas Satan is a liar and the father of falsehood, and "there is no truth in him; when he speaketh, he speaketh a lie out of his own." (*John* 8.44). Everyone, however, is free to follow whichever of the two he prefers—Truth Itself, and be crowned, of the Archliar, and be condemned.

BAPTISM AND AFFUSION

Baptism denotes total immersion of the body into water, just as in dyeing clothes they must be entirely immersed in the dye. Holy baptism is a type of death of the old Adamic man. Sprinkling (aspersion) or merely pouring the water upon the head (affusion) is subversive of holy Baptism and a mockery thereof. The Lord Jesus Christ did not command aspersion or affusion, but **immersion** (baptism). Nor did He say that mere invocation of the names of the Holy Trinity completes Baptism, but that baptism must come first and then the invocation—"...baptizing them in the name of the Father, and of the Son, and of the Holy Spirit." This proves that neither baptism alone apart from the invocation perfects the person baptized, nor the invocation without the baptism, but only both taken together. Hence any contradiction and opposition to the words of the Lord Jesus is a veritable Satanic invention.

Our Lord Jesus Christ was baptized with the baptism of repentance administered by John the Baptist and Forerunner in one mmersion and at the age of thirty, yielding to the law and justice of God the Father, that the Devil might have nothing to accuse Him of. That is why He said to John the Baptist, who sought to avoid baptizing Him: "Suffer it to be so now: for thus it becometh us to fulfil all righteousness." (*Matt.* 3.15). John baptized with one immersion and in the name of the one God, for the Holy Trinity had not yet been revealed. Jesus, however, first observed the Mosaic law and every iota thereof, and afterwards laid down the Gospel law, commanding the Apostles to baptize in the name of the Father, and of the Son, and of the Holy Spirit three times in succession. He did not say, "...baptizing them in the name of the Holy Trinity once," but enunciated the three hypostases separately and distinctly. Nor did He set any limit to the age at which a person may be baptized, or prohibit the baptism of infants.

The holy Apostles put into practice all the laws laid down by Jesus, observing them with exactitude and making no distinction as to the age of the baptized or any attempt to confine baptism to a single immersion, for the set of laws laid down by Jesus are perfect and require to be observed by the faithful, and not to be corrected or to be replaced by others under any pretext whatever. This is why St. Paul commanded the "twelve" who had been baptized with John's baptism to be "baptized in the Name of the Lord Jesus." (*Acts* 19.1-5). This shows that John's single-immersion became useless after the legislation instituted by Jesus.

INFANT BAPTISM

With regard to the age of persons being baptized, we read the following: "And he commanded them to be baptized in the Name of the Lord." (*Acts* 10.48). A trance came upon St. Peter, and, after an oracle had been given to him by God, he went down to Caesarea, preaching Christ to Cornelius and all those roundabout him. While St. Peter was preaching "the Holy Spirit fell on all them who heard the word." Then he commanded them to be baptized. Cornelius was a "devout man and one that feared God with all his house," upon whom the Holy Spirit fell before they had even been baptized with water. Nevertheless, St. Peter, the Spirit-bearing Apostle, commanded that they be baptized with water also, since he evidently judged this to be necessary, and he drew no distinction as to age in regard thereto. (Only once in the history of the Church has the descent of the Holy Spirit preceded the act of baptism; this occurred so that circumcised Christians might be assured that the gift of the Holy Spirit is affused upon heathen too.)

"And when she was baptized, and her household..." (*Acts* 16.15). A certain woman named Lydia, hearing the chosen vessel preach Christ, believed and was baptized, she and her household (i.e., her family and servants). "And he took them the same hour of the night, and washed their stripes; and was baptized, he and all his, straightway," (*ibid.* 33). The keeper of the prison came to believe in Christ as a result of the miracle and the teaching of Paul and Silas, and he and all his were baptized "with all his house." "And Crispus, the chief ruler of the synagogue, believed on the Lord with all his house; and many of the Corinthians hearing, believed and were baptized." (*Acts* 18.8). Thus St. Paul made no distinction as to the age of those baptized, but, on the contrary, with his own hands baptized "the household of Stephanas" (1 *Cor.* 1.16), irrespective of age. Nowhere in his epistles does he prohibit the baptism of infants.

Having then, the holy Apostles as examples, let us imitate them, who not only precisely observed everything that had been decreed by Jesus, but both orally and practically imparted to the Church by tradition the manner in which the sacraments should be performed. Indeed, St. Paul cautions the churches concerning the traditions, saying: "Therefore, brethren, stand fast, and hold the traditions which ye have been taught, whether by word or by our epistle." (2 *Thes.* 2.14; cf. Gal. 1.8 and 1 *Tim.* 6.20).

Arguing from the words of the Lord Jesus in which He said: "He that believeth and is baptized shall be saved" (*Mark* 16.16) and "Go ye, therefore, and teach all nations, baptizing them in the Name of the Father, and of the Son, and of the Holy Spirit" (*Matt.* 28.19), the heretics decry baptism of infants, on the grounds that the infants must first believe and then be baptized. However, a negative conclusion cannot be drawn from the above premises regarding the baptism of infants; rather may it be said that the premises favor it, for Christ made no distinction as to infants. The unbelieving and the idolatrous must first be catechized, believe, and be baptized. Infants, on the other hand, are subject to the will and inclination of their parents, who lead them to put their faith in whatever they themselves believe.

The Logical Conclusion: From positive premises, such as "baptizing them," without other distinction, and "he that believeth and is baptized," likewise without other distinction, whether adult or infant (since the parents believe for their infants, for whom they are responsible), it is not permissible to draw negative conclusions. Yet heretics do draw negative conclusions therefrom, because they violate the laws of reason or leave it out of account altogether. Here is a concrete example from the Bible. Circumcision was a type of Baptism, regarding which a law was given that male infants had to be circumcised on the eighth day after their birth, otherwise they would be subject to God's vengeance. Did the infants of those days have any consciousness or knowledge of the law of circumcision? Of course not.

BAPTISM IS EQUIVALENT TO DEATH

Comparing death and baptism (figurative, or typical, death resulting from Holy Baptism), St. Paul teaches us the following: "Or are ye ignorant that all we who were baptized into Christ were baptized into his death? Therefore we were buried with him through baptism into death, in order that just as Christ rose from the dead through the glory of the Father, so we also may walk in newness of life. For if we have been planted together in the likeness of his death, we shall be also in the likeness of his resurrection." (*Rom.* 6.3-5).

Water is an element and instrument of death. Every living body when plunged into water is drowned and dies; but every living body that is sprinkled with water not only does **not** die, but is even refreshed for the better. Where, then, is there a type of death in sprinkling? Only in the empty heads of the Popes.

"Planted together" is said of two or more grains of wheat sown in the ground and growing together. Our Lord Jesus Christ fell upon the earth like a grain of wheat and died, in order to rise and bear abundance of fruit, as He Himself said of Himself: "Except a grain of wheat fall into the ground and die, it abideth alone: but if it die, it bringeth forth much fruit." (*John* 12.24). In like manner, therefore, we, too, through the trine immersion of Holy Baptism die with and are buried with Christ, and thereby are planted with Him and share with Him in the Resurection.

When we are baptized in the Name of Jesus Christ, we confess that we are worthy of death because of our sins, and, in a way, we die. But when we are merely sprinkled with water, in the name of the Pope—for it was he that commanded sprinkling—we are physically refreshened, but metaphysically we die with him a moral death, and are buried with him, after the death of the body, in the lake of fire and brimstone forever, where the second death is (Rev. 20.14; 21.8); in which case we are separated from Christ forever.

The Apostolic Church was succeeded by the Martyric Church, which for two hundred and fifty years had rivers of blood of its members shed through martyrdom in behalf of Christ by the Caesars of Rome, the holy martyrs of which are estimated at fourteen millions. In the end, however, the blood-thirsty emperors of Rome were overcome through the power of the precious and life-giving Cross, **in hoc signo vince,** the Church being at last freed by Constantine the Great an Apostle-like champion of Christianity.

The Martyric Church was succeeded by the Dogmatic Church of the Holy Fathers which, through seven Ecumenical Synods, settled the faith which had been wavering under the impulse of variable winds—meaning, the heresy of evil spirits, or false teaching. "Wisdom hath built herself a house, and hath set seven pillars underneath as supports." (Prov. 9.1). God hath built His Church (His house), setting Jesus Christ as its foundation and head: "This is my beloved Son, of whom I approve; hear ye him." But the Evil One, after dashing many spirits (teachers) to the ground, raised them up against Christ's Church, introducing many heresies to its detriment and through them combating the Foundation, the Head, the Holy Spirit, the Holy Trinity, the All-holy Virgin, the Sacraments, and, in general, every right doctrine of the Holy Spirit, endeavoring to upset and overthrow it entirely.

But the Lord of the Church, the Holy Spirit, on His part, was not sleeping: from time to time He gathered his children together, the Holy Fathers, through whom He cut off the heretics, locking them out of the Church, and by means of the Dogma settled the wavering faith, and morally regenerated the calumniated Lord Jesus Christ. "Wisdom hath built herself a house, and hath set seven pillars underneath as supports." This prophecy alludes to the Seven Ecumenical Synods.

Originally the Dogma was scattered here and there in the Gospel and the sacred traditions. When the heresies, however, began appearing, the need came in for Synods and Dogmas, for which the heretics are to be blamed whose remains are still extant today and function as weeds. These weeds are not only harmless, but are even useful for the growth of the wheat. Naturally, the heretics of today refuse to abide by Synods and Dogmas, because they themselves are heirs to the doctrines of the founders of their respective heresies and the heretical teachers thereof, going to perdition along with them.

The evil Dragon having failed in his attempt to overthrow the Church of Christ by means of the "gates of Hades," the mouths, that is to say, of the heretics who climbed to high places therein, he afterwards raised up out of the sea and out of the earth the "two beasts," that of the East and that of the West, by means of which he tormented and continues to torment even today Christ's Holy Church, although unable to overthrow it, for it has been built upon a "rock," and it has been prophesied that "the gates of Hades shall not prevail against it" (*Matt.* 16.18).

The violation of the divine law is considered a sin, and it can be remedied by repentance and by execution of the divine law. Non-repentance, on the other hand, encourages the violator in impiety and heresy. Heresy is a perversion of the divine law and of the text of the Holy Scriptures, and as such is considered "blasphemy against the Holy Spirit." The violation is reparable, but the perversion is irreparable. "There is sin unto death,... and there is sin not unto death," says John the Evangelist (1 *John* 5.16-17).

Since we are here speaking of sprinkling (affusion or aspersion), the dogmatic testimony of certain Canons, as well as the opinions of eminent Church Fathers on this subject, must be cited in this connection, so as to bring out the truth more clearly.

The Ecumenical Councils adopted the Gospel, sacred tradition, and the 85 Apostolic Canons as a basis for their decisions against heretics. Accordingly, they first defined the Dogma of the faith by means of the Symbol of Faith (or Creed), and excommunicated from the Church those who did not accept it; afterwards they defined the sacraments (or mysteries, as they are called in Greek) and the duties of the clergy and of the laity by written decisions which they named "Synodical Canons."

SYNODICAL CANONS CONCERNING HOLY BAPTISM

CANON L of the Holy Apostles
and the VII of the Second Ecum. Council

"If any Bishop or Priest shall not perform three baptisms for one initiation, but a single baptism, administered in the death of the Lord, let him be deposed. For the Lord did not say, "Baptize in my death," but, "Go ye, therefore, and teach all nations, baptizing them in the Name of the Father, and of the Son, and of the Holy Spirit." (*Matt.* 28.19).

By virtue of this Canon priests and bishops who do not baptize persons with three immersions are unfrocked, or deposed from the office of the priesthood and deprived of the character and privileges of a clergyman.

"When we were enemies, we were reconciled to God through the death of the Son." (*Rom.* 5.10). "All we who were baptized in Christ Jesus were baptized in his death. Through baptism, therefore, we were buried with him in death." (*Rom.* 6.3-4). We were buried with Him through trine immersion, not through sprinkling or a single immersion.

Dionysius the Areopagite, a contemporary of the Apostles, gives voice to the following divine explanation: "The symbolical teaching, therefore, mystically leads him who is sacredly baptized with the three immersions in the water to imitate the thearchica: death and three-day burial of Jesus the life-giver." And again! "The prelate then baptizes him (the catechumen) with three immersions (submersions and emersions) of the initiate, after calling upon the threefold hypostasis of divine bliss" (that of the Father, and of the Son, and of the Holy Spirit).

Athanasius the Great says: "Just as Christ died, and rose on the third day, so we, too, die and rise again in baptism. For submersing the child in the font for the third time and emersing him, signifies the death and resurrection of Christ."

Basil the Great says: "The sacrament of Baptism, therefore, is completed by three immersions and equal number of invocations... for, as it were, the bodies of the persons being baptized are buried in the water."

St. Chrysostom says: "Just as the womb is to the fetus, such is the water to the believer. Submersion is a sign of dying with, emersion, of rising with."

It follows thence that baptism with three submersions and emersions is of Jesus Christ, but that sprinkling and baptism with a single submersion and emersion are of Satan. John's baptism with a single submersion and emersions was replaced with trine immersion by Christ's legislations—that is to say, with submersion and emersion thrice repeated.

CANON XLVI of the Holy Apostles

"We command that any Bishop or Priest who has recognized a baptism or communion administered by heretics be deposed; for "what concord hath Christ with Belial? or what part hath he that believeth with an infidel?" (Likewise *Canons* XLVII and LXVIII of the Apostles, and *Canon* VII of the Second and XCV of the Sixth.)

These Canons depose any bishop or priest from the priesthood if they accept as correct and true the baptism of heretics (and the same applies to sprinkling to an even greater degree) or the sacrifice offered by them, which is to say, the administration of the sacraments and particularly of the bloodless sacrifice of the Lamb. Since Christ has no concord with the Devil, neither has a believer any portion in the kingdom of God with an unbeliever or a heretic.

CANON XLVII of the Holy Apostles

"If a Bishop or Priest rebaptize anyone that has already been truly baptized, or if he fails to baptize anyone tainted by the impious, let him be deposed, as mocking the Cross and the Lord's death and failing to distinguish a priest from pseudopriests."

This Canon deposes any clergyman who baptizes for the second time one who has been previously baptized in proper fashion, because with the second baptism he is re-crucifying and buffooning the Son of God. It likewise deposes from the priesthood any clergyman who fails to baptize a person that has been baptized by heretical pseudo-priests, since he is thus making sport of the Cross and of the Lord's death as well as of His resurrection.

"Christ being raised from the dead dieth no more; death hat no more dominion over him." (Rom. 6.9.). "All we who were baptized in Christ Jesus were baptized in his death. Through baptism, therefore, we were buried with him in death;... and we have been planted together in the likeness of his death," as St. Paul says. (*Rom.* 6.3-5). But Christ also called death on the cross "baptism, "when He said: "Ye shall be baptized with the baptism that I am baptized with." (*Matt.* 20.22). "But I have a baptism to be baptized with; and how I am straitened until it be accomplished." (*Luke* 12.50). Here He is alluding to His death on the Cross. And elsewhere: "One Lord, one faith, one baptism." (*Eph.* 4.5). Since the Catholic Church is one in dogmatic faith and one in its baptism, how can the baptism of heretics be true, or the sprinkling practiced by the Roman Catholics (Papists)? Such a thing is an utter impossibility.

STRICTNESS — ACCOMODATION — CONCESSION

Both the Apostolical and the Synodical Canons enjoin strictnes and admit of no accomodation or concession as regards Holy Baptism. That is why no accomodation or concession is provided for in any of the Canons.

The Second Ecumenical Council approved accomodation and concession without, however, providing a Canon therefor. It granted recognition to such of the Arians and Macedonians as returned from their heresy and publicly acknowledged their error and received Holy Chrism, without their being rebaptized; they had been properly baptized with three submersions and emersions and in the name of the Father and of the Son and of the Holy Spirit. This alleged accomodation and concession was based upon the Apostolic Canons requiring three immersions. No accomodation, therefore, or concession was really made: the Canons were strictly observed, and that is all. This may be readily seen from the fact that the Ecumenical Synod in question granted recognition to Arians, Macedonians, and the like, in the manner above stated, but denied it to Eunomians and Sabellians unless they were baptized anew, because they had been baptized with only one immersion—the Sabellians, indeed, had perverted even the term "Holy Trinity", and taught that Father, Son, and Holy Spirit were one person.

Illegal accomcdation and concession was made to the Roman Catholics at the time of a great national emergency when the nation was imperiled by the barbarian nations of the East, in the hope of obtaining help from the Popes of the West, who were then at the height of their power, by granting recognition to those who returned from the Roman Catholic Church and received **chrism** alone. Another accomodation made to Roman Catholics was that of calling them **schismatics** instead of heretics after their apostasy and innovations. The greatest illegal accomodation and concession was made during the Council at Florence in 1438-1440 and thereafter, when that accomodation and concession to the Roman Catholics ended in a lamentable tragedy and national calamity from a nationalistic standpoint, but in a victory and triumph of Orthodoxy against Roman Catholicism and its Orthodox sympathizers.

The then rulers of the nation and of Orthodoxy sought mercy and help from the illegal Pope-King! of the West by the illegal accomodation and concession already mentioned, instead of seeking mercy and help from the Universal King Jesus Christ by strict observance of the dogmas and canons of the Church. For this reason the Lord delivered both the nation and the church into the clutches of the wild beast of the East, Mohammed, instead of the wild beast of the West, the Pope-King, because Mohammed enslaved the nation and church only as regarded the body, whereas the Pope-King was and the Pope still is watching for a chance to enslave and corrupt both of them as regards both body and soul.

But those Holy Fathers, too, St. Mark of Ephesus outstandingly, rejected accomodation and concession, and demanded the strict observance of the dogmas, and to them is due that bitter but none the less saving adage, "Better under the broadsword of Mohammed than under the slipper of the Pope!" For this reason the Lord of the Church, the Holy Spirit, delivered the government of Orthodoxy to them, both politically and religiously, under the sway of Mohammed, who, unwillingly and without being aware of it, guarded both nation and church from being spiritually and corporeally devoured by the Pope! And this was due to the fact that the peoples of the East were barbaric in their manners and contrary as to faith, so that assimilation was rendered by nature and position difficult if not impossible; on the other hand, the peoples of the West were civilized in their manners and nearly like us in faith so far as appearances went, so that assimilation was easy if not certain. We have the example of the Greek settlements in Italy and Austria, who were devoured by the Pope through assimilation.

Strictness was advocated at the Council at Florence by Mark Eugenicos (at the 25th session), who said: "We separated from the

3

Latins for no other reason thatn that they are not only schismatics but also heretics. Wherefore, we should not unite with them at all."

Silvester the Ecclesiarch likewise said (*Div.* ix, 5): "The diversity of the Latins is a heresy, and so it was held by our predecessors."

In the ninth chapter of the seventh book of Eusebius it is recorded that one who had been baptized by heretics, upon seeing later how the Orthodox Christians are baptized, wept and could not be comforted, but fell at the feet of St. Dionysius of Alexandria, begging that he baptize him with the Orthodox baptism and saying that the baptism he had received was full of blasphemies and had nothing in common with the Orthodox.

Accomodation can be made where there is no illegality involved. Wherefore St. Chrysostom says: "Accomodation is proper where violation of the law is improper." Legal accomodation was made, as we have already remarked, to heretics who had had trine immersion, and upon their returning to Orthodoxy they were accorded recognition after publicly acknowledging their error and receiving holy chrism, whereas those who had not had trine immersion were baptized, on the ground that they were unbaptized. Another instance of accomodation is that accorded to the Roman Catholics (Latins) at the time of the Council at Florence and thereafter, but it was an illegal accomodation, because the Roman Catholics are unbaptized and wholly heretical and lawless. This accomodation lasted until the fall of Constantinople. For, having been rejected by the sound portion of the clergy and overwhelmingly disapproved by the Orthodox laity, this illegal Council, which had been convoked by force, was condemned and nullified as though it had never been held at all.

St. Mark Eugenicos, having been exiled to the island of Lemnos by Orthodox sympathizers with the Pope, viz., by the newly-elected Patriarch and those of like mind, wrote the following in one of his letters: "... and the majority of the brethren, encouraged by my exile, scourge the scoundrels with criticisms... and drive them from everywhere like vagabonds, refusing to attend mass with them or even to commemorate them as Christians". (he was speaking of the Pope-minded members of the Orthodox Greek Church).

The then Pope-minded (Latin-minded) accorded recognition to Roman Catholics who had only been sprinkled, upon their joining the Orthodox Church, by merely administering the chrism; moreover, they commemorated the Pope, too. But they were deceiving their fellow country men of the Orthodox faith, not daring to tell the truth to their faces. In justification of this evil behavior they asserted that they were following the middle course, citing the Synodical Canon of the Second Ecumenical Synod in the fourth century against the Arians, Macedonians, Sabbatarians, and other heretics, who had been baptized with three submersions and emersions.

In refutation of the Pope-minded, St Mark the aforesaid maintained that the union was effected only formally and not in reality—extrinsically, and not intrinsically—seeing that both dogmatic and ritual differences remained the same as ever, abso_ lute liberty having been granted to each of the Churches as to its own self. Respecting the middle course he said, "nor should this idea deceive anyone; for between two opposite dogmas no middle course can possibly exist. Therefore those who preach the middle course are to be ignored on the ground that they teach nothing stable and definite and certain, but like buskins adhere to both views according to convenience, vacillating from one to the other. Likewise are the Latins to be ignored and shunned entirely, not only as schismatics but also as heretics, he said.

Because they pretended to have made no changes in anything handed down from the Fathers, but did not dare to disclose their own convictions publicly, he reproved their duplicity.

The local council of the Latins held in the Lateran at Rome in A.D. 1215 mentioned in its fourth canon that the Easterners would not perform mass in a place where a Westerner had performed mass antecedently, unless they first performed sanctification for its purification. Afterwards it says that the Easterners rebaptized those joining the Eastern Church, on the ground that they had not had a holy and Apostolic baptism.

It is likewise recorded in the **Nuovo Dizionario** of G. Pivati (Venice 1746-51) that St. Otto baptized with three immersions But fearing, it is said, lest the Latins should disregard the Apostolic Canons and decrees that had been made for the regulation of baptism and violate them, he ordered fonts to be built of marble and placed within the holy temples (churches), rising above ground as high as the knee, so that infants being baptized might be immersed therein with plenty of room. Hence there is such a font to be found in the church of St. Mark at Venice.

"Cursed is everyone that continueth not in all things which are written in the book of the law to do them." (*Gal.* 3.10). And elsewhere: "For whoever shall keep the whole law, and yet offend in one point, he is guilty of all." (*James* 2.10). And again: "Whosoever, therefore, shall break one of these least commandments, and shall teach men so, he shall be called the least in the kingdom of heaven... For say unto you, That except your righteousness shall exceed that of the scribes and Pharisees, ye shall never enter into the kingdom of heaven." (*Matt.* 5.19-20).

Baptism constitutes the first law of Jesus Christ, who said to His disciples: "He that believeth and is baptized shall be saved; but he that disbelieveth (and consequently is not baptized) shall be damned." (*Mark.* 16.16). Which means that belief without baptism will not save the believer. He that believeth and is baptized will be saved; but he that believeth and is **sprinkled** will be **damned,** and let the adherents of sprinkling be not deceived.

Christ said: "He that is not with me is against me; and he that gathereth not with me scattereth abroad. Wherefore, I say unto you, Every sin and blasphemy shall be forgiven unto men, but the blasphemy against the Spirit shall not be forgiven. And whosoever speaketh a word against the Son of man, it shall be forgiven him; but whosoever speaketh against the Holy Spirit it shall not be forgiven him, neither in this world, nor in that which is to come. Either make the tree good, and its fruit good; or make the tree rotten, and its fruit rotten: for the tree is known by its fruit." (*Matt.* 12.30-33). Blasphemy against the Holy Spirit consists in and is the term applied to teaching that is contrary to that of the Prophets and of the Apostles and that of the seven Ecumenical Synods, which were conducted under the guidance of the Holy Spirit and in which the Holy Canons were put in writing

THE THIRD INNOVATION: UNLEAVENED WAFERS

"Jesus therefore said unto them, Verily, verily, I say unto you It was not Moses that gave you the bread out of heaven; but my Father giveth you the true bread out of heaven... I am the bread of life: he that cometh to me shall not hunger, and he that believeth on me shall never thirst... I am the living bread which came down out of heaven: if anyone eat of this bread, he shall live forever;

and the bread which I will give is my flesh, which I will give for the life of the world... Verily, verily, I say unto you, Except ye eat the flesh of the Son of man and drink his blood, ye have no life in you... he that eateth of this bread shall live forever." (*John* 6.32,35,51,53,58).

Through Moses the heavenly Father gave the Jews the manna in the wilderness, which manna they called "bread from heaven." (*John* 6.31). But that bread was the shadow, the type, and the similitude of the true bread. The true bread is Jesus, whom the good Father gave out of heaven, and the eaters of whom shall never die. Having first taught and theoretically explained the food value of the bread that came down out of heaven, he afterwards practically delivered to the Apostles the true bread—His body and His blood—as is related in the following passage: "And as they were eating, Jesus took the bread, and blessed and brake it, and gave of it to the disciples, and said, Take, eat; this is my body." (*Matt.* 26.26).

It was through eating of the forbidden fruit in Paradise that sin and death entered into men, and it is through eating the flesh and blood of Jesus Christ out of the cup that righteousness and life enter and dispel death. The flesh and blood of Jesus is the antidote to death, and by eating and drinketh them man, who is mortal because of the original sin, becomes immortal.

The holy Apostles did as they had been taught by Jesus. They always performed the sacrament of the divine Eucharist by means of (leavened) bread. The church of Christ was instructed by the Apostles how to perform the sacrament with bread, and it observes and will forever observe this rigorous rule unchanged. "And they continued steadfastly in the apostles' doctrine and in communion and in the breaking of bread and in prayer." (*Acts* 2.42). They called the sacrament of the Eucharist breaking of bread and communion.

"And upon the first day of the week (our Sunday), when the disciples gathered together to break bread, Paul conversed with them... And having come up, and having broken bread, and having tasted thereof, and having talked for quite a while until daybreak, he departed." (*Acts* 20:7,11). "For I received from the Lord that which I also delivered to you, that the Lord Jesus on the night in which he was betrayed took bread, and, after giving thanks, brake it, and said. "Take, eat; this is my body, which is broken for you: do this in remembrance of me." (1 *Cor.* 11.23-24). This custom the Orthodox Church strictly keeps and observes, performing the bloodless, sacrifice with leavened bread.

CONCERNING UNLEAVENED WAFERS

"For the first day of the feast of unleavened bread the disciples came to Jesus, saying, Where wilt thou that we make ready for thee to eat the passover?" (*Matt.* 26.17). "And for the first day of unleavened bread, when they were wont to sacrifice the passover, his disciples say unto him, Where wilt thou that we go away and make ready that thou mayest eat the passover?" (*Mark* 14.12). "And the day of unleavened bread came, on which the passover had to be sacrificed. And he sent Peter and John away, saying, Go and make ready for us the passover, that we may eat the passover." (*Luke* 22.7.).

The fifteenth day of the month of March was called the first day of the feast of unleavened bread, because, beginning with this day, all leavened bread disappeared from every Jewish household, and unleavened bread ("matzos") was eaten for seven days. On the evening of the fourteenth day of the same month the paschal lamb was sacrificed, and it was eaten during the night with unleavened bread in accordance with the law's percept. But the Passover was made ready three or four days in advance, or before the day of unleavened bread, on which the lamb was sacrificed and eaten. For this reason the dative case of the Greek word for "first" (day) must be interpreted by the preposition "for" as an expression of a causal relation, and not by the preposition "on" as an expression of a temporal relation. The dative case is equivalent, as a general rule, to the English prepositions "to" and "for"—either the one or the other of which is employed to translate it, according to the context. In the case under discussion it is plain that "for". And not "to" makes sense in English, as well as "on", and in Greek likewise either a causal or a temporal meaning may be attached to the dative case in the sentence above quoted. Which is the true meaning can be inferred only by reference to the context as a whole and surrounding circumstances. If we accept the causal sense as the true one, the meaning becomes: "Because of the first day of unleavened bread," or, "on account of the approach of the first day of unleavened bread, the disciples came to Jesus, and asked Him where He wanted them to get the Passover ready, so that they might eat it on the first day of unleavened bread." But the headless translators of the Holy Scriptures overlooked these facts and relied only on guesswork in making their translations; for this reasons their readers are unable afterwards to make heads or tails of their words. Their mistranslation is inconsistent with the preparation of the Passover, which took place several days before the first day, and not on the first day, for on that day the Passover was ready to be eaten. In order to reconcile the false statement in the English version with the truth of the matter, commentators are compelled to make many absurd assumptions, and become involved in an endless labyrinth of foolish suppositions. The same reasoning, of course, applies to all three of the passages above quoted. In order to convince himself concerning the truth of these conclusions, the reader is advised to consult the Old Testament passages bearing upon the celebration of the Jewish Passover, particularly *Ex.* 12.17-19. The Jewish Passover was sacrificed (celebrated) on the evening of the fourteenth day of March; the preparation for it, however, began on the tenth day of the month and lasted until the thirteenth, which was the eve, or day before the Passover. Nevertheless, it was the custom to say "Passover has come" on the eve of Passover, and not on the day thereof.

Apostolic Canon LXX:

"If any Bishop or Priest or anyone in the list of clergymen fasts with the Jews or celebrates a feast with them or receives from them the gifts of the feast, that is, azymes, or any such thing, let him be deposed. In case he is a layman, let him be excommunicated."

From this also it becomes patent how reprehensible the Latins are, who have made innovations in the sacrament of the Eucharist and have introduced into it the Jewish azymes ("matzos"), or unleavened wafers. That the azymes are an innovation is quite plain. For, from the time of Christ down to the year 1053, the Western Church celebrated mass with leavened bread; in the year just mentioned Pope Leo IX substituted azymes for the first time. The first man to compose the Holy Mass was James the Apostle, and St. Basil extended it, and his extension was further lengthened by St. Chrysostom. All these writers direct the Holy Eucharist to be celebrated with bread.

The infallible Pope uses unleavened bread, instead of leavened, in celebrating the Eucharist, on the strength of the allegation that Christ ate the Passover with unleavened bread in the case under discussion, misinterpreting the passages above quoted and thereby inviting perdition upon himself and his followers. In doing so he rejects or disregards the positive statements of Jesus: "I am the bread," "he that eateth of this bread," "Jesus took the bread... and said,... this is my body," etc., so as to further his heresy and error.

The disciples made ready the Passover on T h u r s d a y the f i f t h day of the week, and ate it in company with Jesus; then went to a place called Gethsemane, where Jesus was arrested by the Pharisees. However, it was the New Passover, or Easter, which they ate, and not the Old, or Jewish, Passover. The Jewish Passover was sacrificed, or celebrated, on the following Friday, the sixth day of the week, in the evening, about six o'clock by the Jewish hour, or twelve o'clock by ours, and was eaten in the night with azymes (matzos), and the following day (Saturday) was called the first day of azymes (unleavened), for it was counted the first and after it came the other six days of azymes.

"Then they led Jesus from Caiaphas to the praetorium (the governor's headquarters, or hall of justice). It was morning; and they themselves (the Pharisees) went not into the praetorium, that they might not be defiled, but might eat the passover." (*John* 18.28).

The scribes and Pharisees did not fear God, and, contrary to the law, they condemned righteous and innocent Jesus to death, but they did fear being defiled by going into the praetorium, which would have prevented their eating the Passover that evening. Though swallowing the camel, they strained out the gnat, lest they swallow it too. The infallible pontiffs of Rome, on the other hand, outview the Pharisees by swallowing the camel without even straining out the gnat; for they eat the Jewish azymes, but observe no law whatever.

The last-quoted passage is further proof that Jesus did not eat azymes and the paschal lamb at the supper of the last evening with His disciples, for that was not the day of azymes and of the Passover. Thus it is plain that they did not eat the "legal" Passover, but the new Passover of the Lord, which they ate with **bread** and **reclining** at the table; whereas, had it been the "legal"

Passover, or Jewish Pasch, they would have been obliged to eat **azymes standing** and with their loins girded. No complaint was made against Jesus and His disciples that they had eaten the Passover reclining, for they did not eat the "legal" Passover at all. The Lamb of God took bread and, having blessed it, said: "This is my body. Take, eat;... do this." Moreover, He sacrificed Himself the next day, Friday, becoming both sacrificer and sacrificial victim in the person of the Lamb. Therefore the bread offered in sacrifice at the Eucharist is in reality the Lamb of God that taketh away the sin of the world; and he that eateth of this bread will live forever.

The Roman Catholics keep the Jewish Passover instead of the Christian Easter, for instead of bread they use unleavened wafers, or azymes, and let them not deceive themselves. Instead of the essence they keep the type and the shadow; instead of grace, the curse of the law. But both the Jews and the Roman Catholics are on the road to perdition, which will surely be their fate unless they repent and embrace Christ. The few Orthodox Christians who join the ranks of the Roman Catholic Church are to be classed with Judas the betrayer and are only inviting their own perdition. Let them beware of hallucination.

Jesus expired upon the Cross the ninth hour of Friday, or about 3 p.m. according to our time of the day. While the Jewish Passover was being celebrated, Jesus was already in His new tomb. His disciples, having scattered out of fear or having hidden themselves in the attic, were groaning in grief, until they heard that immortal reveille announcing: "He is risen; He is not here!"

Consequently, the false supposition that Jesus ate the Jewish Passover with His disciples with azymes, before the advent of the Passover, is proven to be utterly fallacious. Yet upon that supposition the Roman Catholic Papists base their heresy of azymes—the heresy of celebrating the sacrament of the Eucharist with unleavened wafers, and not with (leavened) bread in accordance with the Lord's teaching. Morever, those of our own Orthodox brethren who accept the sprinkling of Roman Catholics joining the Orthodox Church as valid and sufficient to take the place of true baptism (trine immersion) are equally guilty of the azyme heresy of the Pope, since he is the inventor and legislator of both those diabolical institutions; and let them not deceive themselves. The Holy Spirit prophesied with regard to such persons: "I know thy works, that thou art neither cold nor hot: I would thou wert cold or hot. But because thou art thus lukewarm, and neither cold nor hot, I will spew thee out of my mouth." (*Rev.* 3:15-16).

THE FOURTH INNOVATION

The fourth innovation of the Popes is the doctrine that the transubstantiation of the bread and wine into the very body and blood of Christ takes place simply through enunciation of the Lord's words: "Take, eat"; which is an egregious error and heresy and a perversion of the Lord's words, who-first-"blessed" the bread and afterwards invited the disciples to partake thereof by saying, "Take, eat." Likewise, in reference to the cup, He first "gave thanks" and then said, "Drink ye of it all." The false doctrine under consideration is due to the Pope's claim to primacy and infallibility. Once the Papists subscribed to the illogical and diabolical tenet of the Pope's primacy, it was only natural that they should embrace every other foolish doctrine emanating from his infallible and diabolical head, disregarding the word of the Lord because of their own priggery.

THE FIFTH INNOVATION

The fifth innovation of the Popes is that of administering communion in only one kind, excluding the laity from partaking of the cup and allowing it only to the clergy, contrary to the command of the Lord, who said: "Drink ye of it all." They claim that they mix (or soak) the bread (which, however, is not bread but only unleavened wafers in all respects like Jewish matzos) with the wine, and thereby commune the laity. This innovation, too, was inspired by the infernal Dragon, who presented it as a gift to his image—which is to say to the beast rising up out of the earth—since it has no reference to the words of Jesus and does not fulfil His commandment. The Roman Catholics rely upon the Pope and his words, and pay no attention to the Lord's words. But let them listen to what the Holy Spirit prophesies with regard to such persons: "Cursed be the man that trusteth in man, and maketh flesh his arm, and whose heart departeth from the Lord." (Jer. 17.5).

THE SIXTH INNOVATION

The sixth innovation of the Popes is that of Purgatory. According to the Papists, sinful souls (but what soul, besides that of Jesus, is righteous?) enter it after death and are purified through the prayers of the Popes. When, however? Whenever the relatives of the deceased pay the requisite sums, the amount of which depends upon the sins of the deceased and the financial status of the living, unless they are willing to let their beloved be condemned to everlasting punishment. On the basis of this Purgatory the Popes have brought forth their life-saving "indulgences" in behalf of both the living and the dead, which have resulted in the rise of Protestantism with its many heads. Protestantism, in seeking to eradicate heresy by means of its own heresy, and error by means of its own error, and falsehood by means of its own falsehood, contributed rather to the consolidation of the Papal heresy. The Biblical saying, "If the blind lead the blind, both shall fall into the ditch," is applicable to them. If Luther and his followers had adopted the dogma of the Eastern Orthodox Church, neither Protestantism nor Romanism would have been in existence today, but only a single flock under the chief shepherd Christ.

THE SEVENTH INNOVATION

The seventh innovation of the Popes is that decreed a century ago by the Vatican Council as the dogma of immaculate conception of the Theotokos (mother-who-has-given-birth-to God), which asserts that she did not share the original sin—a dogma which is blasphemous, for it represents her as being at the same time Mother and Son, notwithstanding that she derived her substance (hypostasis) from the seed of earthly Adam, having been born of parents named Joach m and Anna.

These are the principal innovations introduced by the Popes and are all due to the Popes' claim to primacy, which caused the separation and the excommunication issued against them by the pastors of the Orthodox Church of Christ.

MINOR INNOVATIONS

But besides the seven major innovations (heresies) and the infallible primacy, the Popes fabricated and introduced other innovations of a lower order, such as, for instance:

1) The use of statues instead of icons (sacred images, or pictures), in imitation of the idolators. The icon, being a picture represents and depicts to the eye the departed **soul**, whereas the statue represents to the touch the **body** of the departed. The Church of Christ handed down the icons from the very beginning, having ousted the statues from the churches. St. Luke, one of the seventy Apostles and the author of the Gospel bearing his name as well as of the Acts of the Apostles, initiated the practice by painting pictures of the Theotokos while she was still alive, which she blessed. The Eastern Church preserved this heritage in spite of the furious war waged by the iconoclasts and notwithstanding the pressure and propaganda put forth by the statuarian Romanists.

2) The celibacy of the clergy, instituted in the sixteenth century by Pope Gregory XIII of Rome, which is not recommended anywhere in the Holy Scriptures or in the Apostolical or Synodical Canons. Everyone is left free to choose marriage or celibacy for himself. The Lord said: "All men cannot receive this saying, but they to whom it is given. For there are eunuchs who were so born from their mother's womb; and there are eunuchs who have made themselves eunuchs for the sake of the kingdom of heaven. He that is able to receive it, let him receive it." (*Matt.* 19.11-12). As a consequence of the law of celibacy of the Papal clergy, the latter fell into malfeasances for which they were subject to no disposal from office when caught in the act, nor are they even now so punished, but only transferred.

For in the Roman Catholic Church the doctrine of the Jesuits that "The end justifies the means" prevails and is practiced. That is to say, whatever they do they do for the glory of God, and therefore it is no sin. Adultery, wars with those who oppose the Holy Pope, etc. are all pardonable, because they are practiced for the glory of God and the subjection of all to the Pope!

3) The change of the Julian calendar by Pope Gregory XIII of Rome in the year 1582 by calling October 5th October 15th. Satan had long endeavored to change the calendar through the agency of many antichrists and astrologers, but had been constantly defeated by the monkery of both the East and the West, aided by those fearful anathemas of the Seventh Ecumenical Synod against all who should attempt to add to or to subtract from the decrees and regulations issued by the Holy Synods. St. Bede, a monk and philosopher (Anglo-Saxon, A.D. 730) stoutly declared:

"The alleged correction of the ecclesiastical calendar is not permissible to anyone." Likewise conscientious astronomers have at various times declared that no Synod should permit a change of the calendar on an astronomical basis, because astronomers never agree in their astronomical calculations.

THE CHANGE OF THE CALENDAR

In the end, however, the aforesaid Gregory ascended the Papal throne (A.D. 1572) and in cooperation with the astrologers J. Stoeffler, Regiomonus, and Aloysius Lilius effected the change, of the calendar, and changed its name to the "Gregorian". But it took 150 years to establish the new calendar in the West, during which rivers of blood were shed, and it is even now acknowledged to be erroneous both from the ecclesiastical and from the scientific points of view by astronomers of the West.

The Orthodox Eastern Church disapproved and condemned and anathematized the Gregorian calendar at three consecutive Synods in Constantinople in A.D. 1583 under the presidency of the patriarchs Jeremiah of Constantinople, Silvester of Alexandria, and Sophronios of Jerusalem; and the second time by the same authorities in the year 1587; and the third under the presidency of Jeremiah of Constantinople, Meletios Pegas of Alexandria, Joachim of Antioch, and Sophronios of Jerusalem.

ATROCITIES OF POPE GREGORY XIII

Pope Gregory XIII is represented by historians of his time as a haughty and corrupt Pope of Rome and as the most bloodthirsty of them all. He reigned during the sixteenth century when rivers of blood were shed both of Protestants and of Roman Catholics because of their apostasy and their attack upon the Pope under the leadership of Luther.

"And the fifth angel poured out his vial upon the throne of the beast; and his kingdom was darkened; and they gnawed their tongues for pain, and they blasphemed the God of heaven because of their pains and their sores; and they repented not of their works." (*Rev.* 16.10-11). Luther attacked the Pope's throne directly, by disputing his authority and legislation; thus the prophecy was fulfilled as to both the peoples of the West.

In the sixteenth century the Papal throne was taken possession of and occupied by means of the broadsword, and fire was constantly burning and charring those who dared to bring any accusation against the Pope. The Popes themselves poisoned their own relatives in order that they might inherit their worldly goods, and they perpetrated every vicious deed against sisters and daughters. They occupied themselves with magic, under the pretext of studying astrology, and on this account were called antichrists even by their own followers.

On the night of St. Bartholomew, A.D. 1575, the Roman Catholics fell upon the Protestants in Paris by deceit and treachery, and killed them while they were attending church and off their guard, for only five days earlier they had confirmed their treaty of peace. The massacre, becoming general, lasted three days. In the houses and streets of the city and in other towns of France they murdered the Protestants in the most fiendish manner "for the glory of God" and His representative the Pope! The dead in Paris alone amounted to some thirty thousands, and in all France some sixty thousands of Protestants were slaughtered without mercy, men and women, old people, children, and infants. The Roman Catholics were not ashamed before men nor did they fear God.

Pope Gregory XIII was so overjoyed at the blood shed on the horrible night of St. Bartholomew, when untold thousands of adults and infants were put to the sword, that he decorated the Roman Catholic murderers as a reward for their deed of atrocity bestowing upon each of them a coin bearing on the one face a likeness of the Pope, and on the other a fiery angel holding in one hand a cross and in the other a broadsword. At the behest of the Pope the day of slaughter was celebrated all over Europe with glorifications, bonfires, and cannon-firing. The Pope himself celebrated mass for the glorification of God, and had a medal struck in honor and memory of that inhuman scene and conducted a litany in Rome as a sign of satisfaction. In Spain, too, priests glorified this achievement of the Roman Catholics (Papists) from their pulpits.

The Holy Scriptures were burned, and Roman Catholics were prohibited from studying them, the Pope having issued his diabolical bull commanding people to "believe, and search not," which is still being circulated among the ignorant and heedless,

and which contradicts the express command of Jesus to the Apo-
sltes, saying: "Search the Scriptures; for in them ye think that ye
have eternal life, and they are they which testify of me." The
Pope's bull also contradicts the command of God our Father,
who told Joshua: "And the book of this law shall not depart out
of thy mouth, and thou shalt meditate (study) therein day and
night, that thou mayest understand all that is written therein;then
shalt thou be prospered and shalt prosper thy ways, and then shalt
thou understand." (Josh. 1.8). And it contradicts the Psalmist
singing: "...and in his law shall he (the godly man) meditate day
and night." (*Ps.* 1.2).

Such, in brief, was the father of the Gregorian modern ecclesiastical calendar. Anyone wishing to learn in detail concerning
the exploits of the Popes and those of the father of the modern calendar in particular, should read: Meletios' **Ecclesiastical History**
of the 14th, 15th, and 16th centuries, and the Introduction to
Chapter VIII of Koumas' **History,** vol. 7 pp. 49-51, as well as
the **History of Romanism** by Rev. John Bowling, A. M., 3rd od,
New York (for the burning of the Holy Scriptures and the command to "believe and search not" see pp. 440ff.). If these works
are inaccessible to the reader, he will do well to refer to the list
given in the footnote on page 12 of this book.

Apostolic Canon VII: "If any Bishop or Priest or
Deacon celebrate the holiday of Easter before the vernal equi-
nox with the Jews, let him be deposed."

Since as a matter of truth the Jews had to celebrate their
Passover first, "and they themselves went not into the praetorium, lest they should be defiled, but might eat the passover,"
and the Lord's resurrection took place later, the Easter which
we now celebrate every year being a type and remembrance thereof, the Canon above quoted was evidently ignored and violated
when the Pope introduced the Gregorian calendar, in consequence
of which the Roman Catholics often celebrate Easter before the
Jewish Passover.

As the fifth innovation after the eight major ones we note
the administration of extreme unction to a sick person on the
point of dying, not for the purpose of promoting the recovery
of his body and soul, but as the last provision for death. The
Roman Catholic priests prefer to have the sick man die, and in
the event that a dying person to whom extreme unction has been

administered survives, they deem it a profanation of the sacrament; and many tales have been told about clergymen of the Roman Catholic faith who strangled those showing signs of life, so as to prevent their holy oil from being polluted—acting, of course, in accordance with their faith.

Here is the text of the Holy Bible from which our Mother Church derived this sacrament of unction: "Is anyone among you ill? let him call in the priests of the church; and let them pray over him, anointing him with oil in the Name of the Lord... and if he have commited sins, they shall be forgiven him." (*James* 5.14-15). Unction is administered by the priests of the Orthodox Greek Church for a person's recovery from illness of body or soul, and not as a preparation for his death.

The foregoing represents in brief the exact truth concerning the Papal Primacy and infallibility, and concerning the innovations of the Pope, both major and minor. Of their primacy and infallibility it may be said that these presumptuous doctrines are on the decline, whereas the other innovations are in full swing. Nevertheless, the Dragonish Papal edifice may be expected to tumble down before long, because it has been built upon sand, as is written: "Therefore whosoever heareth these sayings of mine, and doeth them, I will liken him unto a wise man who built his house upon a rock; and the rain descended, and the floods came, and the winds blew, and beat upon that house, and it fell not; for it was founded upon a rock (which is Christ). And everyone that heareth these saying of mine, and doeth them not, shall be likened unto a foolish man who built his house upon the sand; and the rain descended, and the floods came, and the winds blew, and beat upon that house, and it fell; and great was its fall." (*Matt.* 7.24-25).

All learned persons and students who wish to learn the facts in detail concerning the primacy and innovations of the Roman Catholic (Papal or Romish) Church, should study ecclesiastical history, the writings of the learned, and the confessions of Roman Catholics, and especially the Pedalion of the Orthodox Church; and they will be rewarded with a broader view of the truth.

CANONS SOME APOSTOLICAL AND OTHERS SYNODICAL RESPECTING CLERGYMEN AND LAYMEN

CANON LXV of the Holy Apostles

"If any clergyman or layman join a congregation of Jews or of heretics to pray, let the clergyman be deposed, and the layman be excommunicated."

Many persons, both among the clergy and among the laity, sin by violating this Canon; for anyone that prays in company. with heretics acknowledges in practice that their faith and heresy are commendable. But let them take note of St. Paul's warning: "Be ye not unequally yoked together with unbelievers: for what fellowship hath righteousness with unrighteousness? and what communion hath light with darkness? and what concord hath Christ with Belial? or what part hath he that believeth with an infidel?" (2 *Cor.* 6.14-15).

An infidel and a heretic are in the same category so far as concerns truth and Christ. Yet the heretic is more injurious than the infidel, because he transfigures himself into an angel of light, with a view to instilling his heresy. Accordingly, the Canon deposes the clergyman from the priesthood, and excommunicates (or cuts off) the layman from the body of the Church. Many of the laity, including women as well as men, join the congregations of heretics and pray with them, and afterwards enter an Orthodox church and thoughtlessly partake of communion unworthily and without confessing their sin. The Holy Spirit excommunicates them invisibly, and their end is miserable unless they repent.

CANON LXXII of the Sixth Ecumenical council

"Let it not be permissible for an Orthodox man to take for his wife a woman who is a heretic, nor, on the other hand, for an Orthodox woman to be married to a man who is a heretic. But if such a thing should appear to have been done by anyone of all the clergy, the marriage shall be deemed void, and the unlawful tie shall be dissolved. For immiscibles are not to be mixed, nor must the wolf be yoked together with the sheep, or the portion of Christ with the lot of sinners. If anyone violate what we have enjoined, let him be excommunicated."

By virtue of this Canon any member of the Orthodox Church, whether man or woman, is excommunicated if he or she weds a

4

heretic, unless he or she repents and divorces her or him, or the heretic repents and is baptized in the Orthodox fashion.

So-called mixed marriages—that is, of an Orthodox man with a heterodox woman who is a heretic, or of an Orthodox woman with a heterodox man who is a heretic—are void religiously and invalid in Greece. The whole burden of guilt rests upon the clergyman who blesses such a marriage with crowns. The enforcement of the Canon curbs illegal marriages, whereas the violation of it multiplies the latter. A sorry life and a sorry end will be the fate of the Orthodox member as a result of his mixed marriage with a heterodox woman or man who is a heretic.

CANON LXIV of the Holy Apostles

"If any clergyman is found fasting on the Lord's day or on Saturday, except the one and only Saturday on which it is permissible, he shall be deposed. If any layman be found doing likewise, he shall be excommunicated."

A pious Christian may fast on the other days on the week for the sake of temperance and sobriety, but he must not make a law where there is no law. This Canon is violated more especially by clergymen who impose a three days' fast on those who wish to partake of communion, since there is no law requiring people to fast for this sacrament.

CANON XX of the First Ecumenical Council and XC of the Sixth

"Inasmuch as there are some persons who kneel on Sunday and on the days of Pentecost, it has seemed good to the Holy Synod to declare in favor of keeping everybody in all parishes standing upright while they are rendering prayers to God."

From Holy Easter until the last evening of Pentecost, this Canon tells us, we must **not** kneel while praying, but MUST REMAIN STANDING, as well as on all the Sundays of the year. Sunday is the Lord's day, the day of Resurrection, of gladness, and of rejoicing, not of mourning. There is a proper time for everything. We must not imitate the heathens and heretics, but the Holy Fathers, who framed the Canons and kept them.

CANON LXXVII of the Sixth Ecumenical Council

"That neither church officials nor clergymen nor ascetics

nor any Christian laymen may go bathing in a bathing place with women; for this is the first thing to be condemned among the customs of the heathens. If anybody be caught doing this, in case he is a clergyman, let him be deposed; but if he is a layman, let him be excommunicated."

Those who bathe in bathing places, whether lakes, seas, or rivers, in company with women, if clergymen, are deposed; if lay Christians, they are excommunicated. This mode of bathing is the invention of idolaters. It is an act originating from immoral principles and involves an indecent exposure of the body. Nudity of the body is a sign of moral insensibility of the soul; for the body acts and moves in accordance with the desires and volitions of the soul. Before the advent of Christ God's chosen people, the Jews, imitated the idolatrous heathens in all their evil works; after the advent of Christ God's chosen people, the Christians, imitate the heathens in all their evil works (among the heathens are included all Christians who are impious or have apostatized from the Orthodox faith!)

CANON IX of the Holy Apostles

"All the faithful who come in and listen to the Scriptures but do not stay for prayer and Holy Communion, are to be excommunicated as causing disorder."

This Canon clearly states that if any member of the Church comes to church and merely listens to the recital of the Holy Scriptures (i.e., all the psalms and hymns and extracts that have ben taken from the Holy Scriptures) without remaining to partake of Holy Communion, he must be excommunicated on the ground that he thereby contributes to disorder. But it also puts a gag in the mouths of all who out of ignorance and prejudice demand a three days' fast from those wishing to partake of the sacrament of Holy Communion, since this Canon makes no exception whatever for the twelve-day period of Christmas and the resplendent week of Resurrection beginning with Easter when all kinds of food are eaten. The Canons of the Church are to be obeyed in preference to the prejudices of ignorant persons, whatever be their station or position.

How long are the Holy Canons to be trampled underfoot by the guilty? For, having disregarded the commandments of God, the Holy Canons, they persist in the prejudices and ignorance of their predecessors; "they bind heavy burdens and grievous to be borne, and lay them on men's shoulders; but they themselves will not move them with their finger. But all their works they do to be seen by men." (*Matt.* 25.4-5). What Canon gives the sacrificing priest the right to sacrifice and consume the Holy Cup without having previously fasted, yet imposes a three days' fast before Holy Communion on the Christian layman who contributes to the support of the Church? None! Absolutely none. Nevertheless, the ignorant, prejudiced, and hypocritical violators of the Holy Canons impose canons of their own on the congregation. "Woe unto you, scribes and Pharisees, hypocrits! for ye shut up the kingdom of heaven against men: for ye neither go in yourselves, neither suffer ye them that are entering to go in." (*Matt.* 25.14). For through the illegal law of fasting you deprive God's people of the heavenly bread, of the heavenly good, the body and blood of our Lord and God and Savior Jesus Christ, of whom man has need in order to be saved and not perish.

CANON XLII of the Holy Apostles

"Let any Bishop or Priest or Deacon that plays dice or gets drunk be either suspended or deposed."

CANON XLIII of the Holy Apostles

"Let any subdeacon or reader or cantor so guilty (as stated in the foregoing Canon) be either suspended or excommunicated; any layman so guilty shall be excommunicated."

Both the foregoing Canons prohibit games of chance like dice and cards, drunkenness, etc., well as carousals; betting on horse races comes under the same category. The fifty-fifth Canon of Laodicea decrees that neither church officials nor clergymen nor laymen are allowed to hold banquets through the contributions of many persons for such a purpose (as is done in the case of modern picnics, balls, etc.). The sixty-ninth Canon of Cathargene commands Christians to cease holding banquets, balls, and games in commemoration of martyrs and saints. The thirty-fourth Canon of the Seventh Ecumenical Synod prohibits Christians from eating and drinking to the accompaniment of musical instruments and whorish and wanton songs.

The ancient Greek idolators committed all kinds of

excesses during the feasts of their gods (idols). The governing councils presiding over the churches of the Greeks of today imitate them to a certain extent by holding balls, theatrical shows, and picnics on Sundays and holidays with a light conscience and under the pretext of providing for charitable needs and meeting the heavy expenses of the holy temples (churches). In other words, they sacrifice to d e m o n s and celebrate for the sake of money. It is a rule of logic that no good results from a bad act. They conduct themselves as described in the Lord's words: they make His Father's house a house of merchandise. On this account, God, seeing the failure of Christians to repent, has incited all nations to mutual massacre over the whole face of the earth, until they repent and return to the Lord Jesus Christ and submit to Him.

CANON XLIV of the Holy Apostles

"Let any Bishop or Priest or Deacon demanding interest of borrowers be either suspended or deposed."
This Canon needs no explanation.

CANON XLV of the Holy Apostles

"If any Bishop or Priest or Deacon prays together with heretics, let him be excommunicated; but if he has allowed them to act as clergymen in any capacity, let him be deposed."
This Canon is likewise intelligible to all and needs no further explanation.

CANON XXV of the Holy Apostles

"If any Bishop or Priest or Deacon be found guilty of fornication or perjury or theft, let him be deposed (from the priesthood), and not be excommunicated. For the Bible says: "He shall not take vengeance twice on the same count.' (O.T.) Other clergymen shall be treated likewise."
This Canon, too, is self-explanatory. By "other clergymen" is meant subdeacons, readers, and church singers.

CANON XXIX of the Holy Apostles

"If any Bishop acquire his office by means of money, or any Priest or Deacon do so, let him and the one who ordained him both be deposed, and be cut off altogether from the society of Christians, as was Simon by me, Peter."

Simony is the greatest sin, exceeding even that of Judas the betrayer. For this reason the present Canon deposes and cuts off, or excommunicates entirely, both the one ordained and the one ordaining for the sake of money, because they buy and sell the Holy Spirit for money. Canons II of the Fourth Ecumenical Synod and XXII of the Sixth likewise depose and excommunicate those ordaining and those ordained for money. But anyone who steals money belonging to parishes (communities) is also called a simoniac. St. Chrysostom deposed nine bishops who had been promoted to the bishopric in consideration of money.

CANON XXX of the Holy Apostles

"If any Bishop shall acquire a church by making use of temporal rulers, let him be deposed and excommunicated, as well as all who are associated with him."

This Canon deposes a bishop who has acquired an episcopacy or cathedral through political influence and in violation of the Canons, as well as all his assistants.

CANON LIV of the Holy Apostles

"If any clergyman be caught eating in a tavern, let him be excommunicated, unless it be in a wayside inn where he is stopping as a matter of necessity."

This Canon is plain enough.

CANON LV of the Holy Apostles

"If any clergyman insults a Bishop, let him be deposed. For "thou shalt not speak foul words against a ruler of the people. "

This Canon is likewise plain to everybody and requires no comment.

CANON LIX of the Holy Apostles

"If any Bishop or Priest fail to provide necessities when one of the clergy is in want, let him be excommunicated. If he persists in doing so, let him be deposed, as having killed one of his brethren."

This Canon needs no interpretation. Yet examples of such cases are constantly being met with. The bishop is a servant of Christ; the clergy are his relatives. A bishop is not permitted to keep money in the bank, and upon his death everything in his possession reverts to his ecclesiastical office. That is what is required of every pious bishop. For in the life to come our judge will be Christ and our accusers those whom we have wronged.

CANON LXX of the Sixth Ecumenical Council (Concerning Women)

"Let it not be permissible for women to talk during Holy Mass, but in accordance with the words of Paul the Apostle, 'let your women remain silent. For it has not been permitted them to talk, but to obey, as the law directs. If they wish to learn anything, let them ask their husbands at home.' "

"As in all churches of the saints," says Paul the Apostle, "in the churches let your women remain silent. For it has not been permitted them to talk, but to obey, as the law directs. If they wish to learn anything, let them ask their husbands at home." (1 *Cor*. 14.33-35).

"Let the women learn quietly with all subjection. But I suffer not a woman to teach, nor to exercise authority over a man, but to be quiet. For Adam was formed first, and then Eve. And Adam was not deceived, but the woman having been deceived became at fault. But she shall be saved through childbearing, if they abide in faith and love and sanctity with sobriety." (1 *Tim*. 2.11-15).

According to the words of this Canon and according to the words of St. Paul, women are prohibited from teaching either in holy temples (churches) or outside thereof, for St. Paul does not mean by "church" the temple itself, but a "congregation of people" anywhere; and still more are they prohibited from chanting either in a choir of their own or along with men.

"For it is a shame for women to talk in church." (1 *Cor*. 14. 35). This means that women should keep silent in church, and out of church wherever there is a congregation of people. The fact that the word **talk** is used here, and not the word speak, controverts and overthrows the allegation put forward by some persons that only teaching is forbidden to women, but not chanting; for talk includes any sort of vocal utterance, and not merely articulate speech. In fact, women are not allowed to let their voice be heard at all within the sacred temple of the church. They may, of course, sing and chant in their hearts praises and blessings to God, but not with their lips.

Before God formed Eve, He said: "It is not good that man should be alone; let us make for him a helper meet for him." (*Gen.* 2.18). This means that woman was created, not to rule man, but to help him and to be ruled by him. Woman is a teacher of every virtue by word and deed within her own province at home; but she is not allowed even to speak or sing within the sacred precincts of the church. Woman's job is to bear children and rear them in the belief and love of God, to uphold the sanctity and sobriety of marriage, and to shun adultery as a thing that is odious to God. By so doing she will be saved, and not otherwise; by leaving this path and failing in these duties, she invites perdition.

"If anyone think himself a prophet or a spiritual agent, let him acknowledge that what I write unto you are commandments of the Lord. But if anyone is ignorant, let him be ignorant." (1 *Cor.* 14.37-38). A true prophet or teacher or spiritual agent has the spirit of Christ and does not disagree with Christ's Apostle; he easily discerns and believes that St. Paul's commandments are commandments of Christ. Whoever, on the other hand, does not discern and believe this, yet thinks that he is a prophet or a spiritual agent, is merely deluding himself; he is a false prophet lacking the spirit of Christ.

Teaching and chanting are inconsistent with the nature and destiny of a Christian woman, just as are the priesthood and the bishopric. Eve, the woman formed by God, was the first to teach Adam once, in Paradise, and she ruined everything; that is why women are forbidden to talk in churches. The greatest adornment of women is silence. Let their example be Mary, the New Woman and Child of God, who alone has the honor of having had her speech recorded in history and handed down in the ninth ode of the Church; this refers to her speech and that of Elizabeth. Therefore let Christian women emulate her. The ancient idolaters had priestesses to officiate at the altars and in the temples of idols in which demons were worshiped; and hence it is that deluded heretics derived this impious custom of theirs of letting women teach and sing and govern in their churches. Shall we Orthodox Christians imitate them? By no means!

It is recorded in the **Ecclesiastical History** of Eusebius (BookVII, Chapter 30) that a council of bishops met in Antioch in the third century after Christ from various cities for the purpose of trying Paul the bishop of Samosat, who was rather a sophist and magician than a bishop and who, in addition to other heresies, had introduced a choir of women into the church of Antioch. That council addressed a letter to bishops Dionysius of Rome and Maximus of Alexandria containing the following phrases: "Having suppressed the psalms to our Lord Jesus Christ on the pretext that they are modern psalms and the writings of modern men, who is preparing women to chant to himself in the midst of the church on the great day of Easter whom one would **shudder** merely to listen to."

Women were never permitted to teach or to chant in the church along with the sacred cantors or in a choir of their own. Female choirs are an unexampled innovation involving many perils and capable of leading to many scandals, for woman's voice is more attractive and more pathetic than man's. The appearance of women in the church choir constitutes a stumbling block; for the eyes and ears of the congregation are at once turned to them, and, becoming intoxicated with the sight and sound of the highstrung melodramatic voices of women, they are languorously effeminated in mind and rendered incapable of enjoying the modest and contrite songs of the Church; thus the church choir gradually becomes transformed into a theatrical chorus!

Canon LXXV of the Sixth Ecumenical Synod decrees the following with reference to church choirs: "It is our wish that those who come to church to chant should neither employ disorderly yelling and strain their natural voices to scream, nor recite anything inappropriate and not suited to a church, but that they should offer such psalmories with great care contrition to God, who listens and looks on in secret." "The children of Israel shall be reverent," saith the sacred saying (Lev. 15.31).

The holy Liturgy and sacred hymnody presented in church has the purpose of offering prayers to propitate God for our sins. Whoever prays and supplicates should be of humble and contrite mind; yelling indicates rudeness and irreverence of mind. But voices and faces of female choirs and the psalmody of European quartets represent a theatrical mind rather than a modest ecclesiastical mind. What is it that is unsuited to the church? Effeminate songs (melodies) and trills (which means the same thing as the warbles of old) and an excessive variety of tones that inclines to worsh songs, Zonaras, an interpreter of the Canons, says.

The children of Israel after Christ are the pious Christians, who should be imbued with fear of God and reverence while within the church. God is not pleased with variety of melodies and voices, but with contrition and repentance of the heart. This is easily understood when we remember that man is pleased to listen to melodies and to look at pretty faces, whereas God looks into man's soul in the depths of the heart and delights in its reverence, which is manifested by **humbleness** of behavior.

THE TRUE CATHOLIC DOCTRINE OF SALVATION

"He saith unto them, But whom say ye that I am? And Simon Peter answered and said, Thou art the Christ, the Son of the living God. And Jesus answered and said unto him. Blessed art thou, Simon Barjona: for flesh and blood hath not revealed it unto thee, but my Father which is in heaven. And I say also unto thee, That thou art Peter, and upon this rock I will build my church; and the gates of hell shall not prevail against it. And I will give unto thee the keys of the kingdom of heaven; and whatsoever thou shalt bind on earth shall be bound in heaven: and whatsoever thou shalt loose on earth shall be loosed in heaven." (*Matt.* 16: 15-19).

The Father of Christ revealed to Peter that Christ was the Son of the living God, and not what other men thought about Him, who thought Christ to be John the Baptist, or Elias, or Jeremiah, or as one of the prophets. And Christ supplementing the divine revelation made to Peter, says to him that for this reason he was named Peter, he who was formally called Simon son of Jona—that he knew the rock of faith and became the foundation stone of the holy structure and the fact that upon this rock of faith Christ will build His own Church, which the ruler of darkness will fight with all his might, but shall not prevail against it.

(The effectiveness of the above passage in Greek lies in the etymology of the name **Peter** meaning **of rock.**)

Thus every man who knows and confesses Christ as Peter did to be the Son of the living God, becomes **petros** (like rock) that is a rock useful toward the building of the Church all the members of which possess the same essential characteristic, of confessing Christ as the Son of the living God, perfect God, begotten of true God without time, and perfect man born within time of the Holy Spirit and the Virgin Mary according to the testimony of the Evangelists. He who does not believe and testify this does not become **petros** nor a member of the Church of Christ. And he moreover, who denies this testimony, crumbles away from the divine structure or is cut off from association with the Church because he has lost the most essential asset of membership. Therefore the stone upon which Christ promises to build his Church is the confession of Peter, the truth revealed to him by the heavenly Father which abides for ever, the truth which gives birth to Peters and the stones of the divine structure. But the Papists destroy this scriptural passage toward their own damnation arguing sophistically and erroneously that Christ promised Peter to build upon the latter's persons His Church; and the phrase "upon this rock" which clearly signifies the confession of Peter they interpret **upon thee Peter.** And by heaping up more falsehoods upon this one they build up the system of their diabolical heresy through which Satan has attempted the overthrow of the orthodox Church but failed totally; for falsehood is not strong enough to overcome truth. The foundation of the Christian Church in Christ and Peter's testimony. Upon this foundation the apostles have built the once Holy Catholic and Apostolic Church of God, as Peter also testifies in his first Catholic Epistle saying: To whom coming as unto a living stone, disallowed indeed of men, but chosen of God and precious, ye also, as living stones are built up a spiritual house, an holy priesthood, to offer up spiritual sacrifices acceptable to God by Jesus Christ. Wherefore also it is contained in the scripture, Behold, I lay in Sion a chief corner stone elect, precious: and he that believeth on him shall not be confounded." Behold the living stone, the chosen, the precious the corner stone upon which Apostle Peter built the church; behold too the living stones placed upon the Foundation stone of the structure and constituting God's spiritual house within which holy priests offer acceptable sacrifices to God through Jesus Christ. But the Papists of Rome, after repudiating this doctrine of Apostle Peter, boast that they are his only successors, thus deluding themselves and others and bound toward perdition. But this delusion of theirs we have reproached in our work which has been fully reprinted under the title **Memoir of the Nature of the Church of Christ** and whoever wishes may find therein the reproach. But the prophetic statement of Christ regarding the Church to be built upon the testimony of Peter "And the gates of hell shall not prevail against it" has received full historic proof; because since the beginning of the foundation and organization of the Church, Satan's attacks out of the gates of Hell, against the Church and its basic truth for the purpose of destroying them, have proven powerless either toward shaking the foundation. or toward tearing dow the super-structure on the foundation. And the well founded and fighting Church shall prevail against the gates of hell, and after finally overcoming the enemy will imprison him in the place whence he attacked her. The invincible Church will prove victorious through sheer strength over her bitter enemy and will eventually wipe out his power and authority from the face of the earth.

"And I will give unto thee the keys of the kingdom of heaven: and whatsoever thou shalt bind on earth shall be bound in heaven: and whatsoever thou shalt loose on earth shall be loosed in heaven."

The kingdom of heaven has a door which closes and opens, and the door has keys by which it is opened and closed. But what is the door to the kingdom of heaven, and what are the keys that open and close it. The door to the kingdom of heaven is Christ as He says: "I am the door: by me if any man enter in, he shall be saved, and shall go in and out, and find pasture." This door is opened to those who will repent and bring forth fruit worthy of repentance, but it is closed to the unrepentant and unbelieving. And the keys which open and shut this door are the power to bind and loose men's sins. He who has been granted remission of sins by the one who has the authority to do so, enters freely through the door opened for him; whereas he who has not been granted forgiveness does not enter, the door being closed to him. The power to forgive sins was possessed by Christ who exercised it by announcing to those who approached Him in faith the remission of their sins, and by saying "Child be of good cheer, thy sins are forgiven thee." This power Christ, after his resurrection imparted to his own disciples by breathing upon them and saying "receive ye the Holy Ghost: whose soever sins ye remit, they are remitted unto them; and whose soever sins ye retain, they are retained." Then Peter with the other disciples received the keys of the kingdom which Christ promised to give him after his testimony of the truth. The Father showed Peter the door of the kingdom of heaven; and the Son fulfilling the work of the Father gave Peter the keys for opening and closing the door, for ushering in or keeping out those whom he judged worthy or unworthy of admittance. But Peter was not the only one who received from the Father the knowledge of the door nor was he the only one to whom Christ gave the keys for opening and closing it. Christ praying to His Father says: "O righteous Father the world hath not known thee; but I have known thee and these have known that thou hast sent me." And Peter answering Christ says: "Lord to whom shall we go? Thou hast the words of eternal life. And we believe and are sure that thou art the Christ, the Son of the living God." Obviously Peter testifies to a common knowledge of the faith in Christ among the disciples and does not boast that he alone knew and believed in Christ. Therefore he received the keys in common with the other disciples, no one disciple being given the keys individually. But those who distort the Scriptures toward their own perdition, those who have misinterpreted the **rock of faith**, and have built the house of their heresy on false foundation, have also misinterpreted the keys of the kingdom and commercialized them toward filling their purse. The self-elected successors of Peter have become the exclusive and only heirs to the keys of God's kingdom, and the only possessors of the authority to bind and loose and to usher in and put out of Paradise those they wish. And they wish to usher in those who give them silver and gold, whereas Peter excludes from the kingdom of heaven those who offer him silver and gold according to the following proof. The book of **Acts of the Apostles** record that Simon the sorcerer seeing that the Apostles imparted the Holy Spirit through the laying of their hands he offered them money saying: "Give me also this power, that on whomsoever I lay hands, he may receive the Holy Ghost." But Peter said unto him. "Thy money perish with thee, because thou hast thought that the gift of God may be purchased with money. Thou hast neither part nor lot in this matter: for thy heart is not right in the sight of God." Behold, Peter, the key-master of God's kingdom excluded Simon the sorcerer from it for offering silver to the former. But his self-termed successors usher the one offering them the most silver farthings into Paradise. And what may be gathered logically from this contrast? That the keys of Peter are different from those that the Papists hold in their hands. The keys of the latter being different from those of Peter open and close an opposite door— the door of hell and death. And those who give silver to them in order to enter Paradise, enter the Tartarus of eternal damnation whereas these who turn away and flee from the Papists, get farther from the door and entrance which ushers all that enter through it, to everlasting perdition.

Speaking more simple—Christ established His Church on the Confession of St. Peter (Petra) in Greek meaning a Great Rock, and Christ is the Rock of our salvation. The Romish Church established its claim on the person of St. Peter. Therefore, they worship St. Peter more than God, and look to the Pope for their salvation and wage continual war upon Christ's true people everywhere with a view to world-wide domination to rule the Church and Politics in every country and to bring down ruin on all nations.

THE PROTESTANT DOCTRINE OF SALVATION

Note: The original text in English:

(*Heb.* 10.13.14): "But he, having offered one sacrifice for sins to be made continuously, sat down on the right hand of God."

"For by one offering he hath perfected them continuously that are sanctified."

King James Version of the same:

"But he, when he had offered one sacrifice for sins for ever, sat down on the rigth hard of God;"

"For by one offering he had perfected for ever them that are sanctified."

The Greek word here translated in both the Revised and the King James Version by "forever" (which means "everlastingly"), merely denotes "continuously" or "continually" (the distinction between which may be disregarded here, since the Greek word does duty for both). Hence the entire question as regards the meaning of this word in general is whether or not it ever has the meaning of "forever"; and to this question anyone who knows Greek as his mother tongue can answer quite definitely and positively that the word **never** has such a meaning. Hence it is evident that the passage above quoted have been woefully mistranslated into English. The Douay Version used by the Roman Catholics is equally at fault in the above passages, although differently worded and punctuated, since it, too, says "forever" in both cases.

Heretical translators and their followers insist that only the sacrifice on the Cross can save one, and that the sacrifice offered in the cup is made with bread and wine in remembrance of the other but without transubstantiation. The Orthodox Church of Christ, however, firmly believes that the sacrifice offered once on the Cross by the Lamb of God, is **continually** repeated on the altars of the Orthodox churches through transubstantiation of the bread and wine in the cup in consequence of its change into the very body and the very blood of Christ by reason of the blessing and the invocation of the Holy Spirit by the priest sacrificing and the same, since Christ Himself said, and made it a law, that this should be done **continually**. This is proved by the following words of the Gospel : "Take, eat; this is my body, which is broken for you." (1 *Cor.* 11.24). "Drink ye all of it; for this is my blood of the new testament which is shed for you and for many for the remission of sins." (*Matt.* 26.27). As regards those who deny or dispute this saving law of life, He said: "Verily, verily, I say unto you, except ye eat the flesh of the Son of man, and drink his blood, ye have no life in you." (*John* 6.53). This furnishes a clue to the interpretation of the passage, "For by one offering he hath perfected them continuously that are sanctified." How are those who are daily born into the world sanctified? Through the sacrifice of the bread and wine that are in the cup. In other words, the sanctification due to the sacrifice on the Cross is **continued** by the repeated sacrifice that takes place through the sacrament of the Eucharist.

APPENDIX

The propitiatory sacrifice of Jesus on the Cross eliminates or abolishes death from the entire human race through the common resurrection of all men in the day of universal judgment that will attend His second advent. Holy baptism, on the other hand, removes original sin and personal sins only from those who are baptized with the perfect baptism of trine, or threefold, immersion (not the so-called trine aspersion, or sprinking, substituted for it by heretics). Personal sins committed **after** baptism are remitted through due repentance and continual sacrifice in the form of bread and wine administrated in the cup, and through the blessing of transubstantiation into the very body and blood, sanctifying those who partake thereof perseveringly.

Baptism connotes spiritual rebirth. In order that a person who has been born only in the flesh may be reborn and perfected he needs the proper spiritual nourishment, which is the body and blood of Christ given in the cup. Otherwise no true rebirth accrues to the soul of the person born only in the flesh. The study of the written word of God without the nourishment afforded by the mystery, or sacrament, of the Eucharist, imbues the mind with self-conceit, winding up in heresy or unbelief.

A TESTIMONY OF CONVERSION TO CHRIST

From the newspaper *Patris*, of the island of Syros, Greece, dated January 10th 1869, we quote the following paragraph (translated into English):

"James Chrystal, a professor of Greek, Latin and English, as well as a minister, preacher, and author, who came here from New York City, has been baptized of his own accord by Archbishop Lycurgus by three total immersions, after reciting the Orthodox Christian Creed in Greek, Latin, and English by himself. The prefect, K. G. Dracopoulos, stood up for him as godfather in the presence of a large throng of witnesses on January 6, 1869."

From a pamphlet by the same author, James Chrystal, entitled "Baptism and the Original Mode." we excerpt the following portions pertaining to baptism as worthy of note:

BAPTISM AND THE ORIGINAL MODE
By
James George Chrystal

The word *Baptize* is derived from the Greek language, and is only changed a little to agree with the English tongue in pronunciation. The Greek word is Baptizo, and the Ordinance of Baptism in the New Testament is aways referred to by the use of this word. We will introduce lexicons to define it.—

Liddell & Scott—"Baptizo, To dip repeadly."—Greek-English Lecixon.

James Donnegan—"Baptizo, To immerse repeadly into a liquid."—Greek and English Lexicon.

John Parkhurst—"Baptizo, From Bapto, to dip, immerse or plunge in water."—Greek and English Lexicon, Third Edition.

E. A. Sophocles—"Baptizo, To dip, to immerse to sink. Note—There is no evidence that Luke and Paul and the other writers of the New Testament put on this (word) meaning not recognized by the Greeks."—Greek Lexicon.

Edward Robinson—"Baptizo is frequentative in form. Note —Greek writers from Plato on used Baptizo, everywhere to sink, to immerse, to overwhelm either wholly or partially."—Greek and English Lexicon.

Hermann Cremer—"Baptize, The peculiar New Testament use of the word to denote immersion, submersion, for a religious purpose."—Biblico Theological Lexicon, Translated from the German.

Liddel & Scott's is the standard Greek and English Lexicon, and all the others quoted are held in high esteem by scholars. They all define Baptizo as meaning to dip, to immerse, to plunge, and say that it is frequentative in form and denotes repeated actions, and this is the meaning which the Universal Church has always attached to the word, and exhibited in its practice; that is, Trine Immersion.

The history of Baptism is a long history and includes many particulars which are of no relative importance in deciding which is the authorized and primitive mode. The aim of this appendix is to present the evidence which confirms the original mode.

A GLANCE AT THE HISTORY OF BAPTISM

Originally, Baptism was administered for the remission of sins. It was an act in preparation for the gift of the Holy Spirit. This in turn advanced the believer on to the Rebirth, the being born again, which will reach its completion, in the resurrection of the just.

The sciptures seem to make no clear distinction between begetial, begotten, rebirth and being born again. The influence of each, so far as the present life is involved, is about the same, except the being born again certainly is not completed until the new body is received in the resurrection of the just. Thi would exclude many of the extravagant claims set up in the third and fourth centuries of church history. It is enough to know that baptism is a figure or symbol of burial with Christ into death, and arising therefrom to walk in newness of life.

Occasionally, children became dangerously sick who had not been baptized. They were given the rite by pouring water over them three times, and this was called "divine compend" baptism.

The persuasion of many Gentiles to embrace the Christian Faith included learned men and philosophers. Original sin, immortality of the human soul and like teaching saw no difference between the infant and the adult in the hereafter. Baptism was stoutly upheld as necessary for salvation, and therefore the infant needed baptism to save it; to take away sin and come under the remission of sins by the blood of Jesus Christ. Even the virus of sin was made actual with the infant, that no one was free from pollution for the length of one day.

The Eastern Church never departed from the primitive practice of three dip immersions. Infant baptism continued, but was given in the trine immersion.

Little was said about the mode of baptism during the first century, because the practice of trine immersion was general and there was no controversy.

Eunomius, an opponent of the teaching on the Trinity introduced a single immersion into the death of Christ. This was about 360 A.D. It had no known connection with the single immersion performed in the use of the three names now common.

Single immersion was introduced in Spain under the advice

of Gregory the Great. The Catholics of Spain sought a different practice because the Spanish Arians practiced the primitive mode, and Gregory authorized the change, altho the practice in Rome was the trine immersion. Gregory's grant to the Spanish Catholics was endorsed by the Council of Toledo, in 633 A.D. There is no known historical connection between this practice and the origin of the Baptist single immersion centuries later.

During the life of Jesus, the king of Armenia, in Asia embraced Christianity and gave it to his people, and three dip immersion has continued in the Armenian church to the present.

The churches of Asia have continued the three dip immersion from the Apostles to the present.

St. Paul planted Christianity in Macedonia and Greece with the three dip immersion and it continued to be the general practice to the present time.

St. Mark established Christianity in Egypt about 55 A.D. and the church with its three dip immersion has continued to the present.

The first notable instance of sprinkling or pouring as a substitute for the regular three dip immersion was in the life of Novation who flourished in 250 A.D. He was dangerously sick and water was poured upon him as a saving rite. He recovered and became prominent as a leader of a schism.

About 37 A.D. Joseph of Arimathea, who begged the body of Jesus (*Matt.* 27 :58) and laid it in his own new tomb in Jerusalem established a colony of Christians in England. The three dip immersion was established there and continued to be the regular mode till the 16th century.

In the fifth century, Gregory the Great sent St. Austin to England to bring the churches of Britain and England under the Roman Catholic Communion. St. Austin found the regular three dip immersion then practiced in the Catholic Church of Rome.

Christianity was established in Russia in 866 A.D., and became the state religion and three dip immersion has always been the Orthodox baptism of the Russian church.

Acs 8 : 35-38 speaks of the baptism of the Eunuch, an Ethio_pian official, by Philip. The Ethiopians have kept a form of Christianity to the present time and they have the three dip immersion.

This appendix is printed to present the true and original

mode of Baptism as seen in history and present practice in the homelands of the Christian faith, for the benefit of any it may concern, seeking to know the original mode.

The writer does not assume to sit as a judge before the Lord on the virtue of the substitutes or compend and clinical baptism introduced from time to time. But it is our privilege to encourage all candidates for baptism to obtain the three dip immersion that has come down from the primitive Church.

HISTORICAL QUOTATIONS

ST. DIONYSIUS the Areopagite. Acts 17:34. From Writing ascribed to him—"The total hiding or covering by means of water is fitly taken as an image of the death and burial (of Jesus). The symbolic teaching therefore mystically instructs him who is baptized, according to the sacred rite, to imitate by three immersions in the water, the death and burial for three days and nights of Jesus the Life-giver."

ST. AUGUSTINE, from writings under his name—"After you made the profession of your faith, we plunged your head three times in the sacred fount. For rightly you were thrice dipped who have received baptism in the name of the trinity."

TERTULLIAN—Born about A.D. 150. "I shall begin with baptism. When we are going to enter the water, but a little before in the presence of the congregation and under the hand of the president, we solemly profess that we disown the devil, and his pomp, and his angels. Hereupon we are thrice immersed, making a somewhat ampler pledge than the Lord has appointed in the Gospel." "Lastly, He commands them to baptize into the Father and the Son and the Holy Ghost, not into a unipersonal God. And indeed it is not once only, but three times, that we are immersed into the Three Persons, at each several mention of Their names."—(Oxford Translation.)

CYRIL—Born about 315. "Ye were led to the pool of Devine Baptism as Christ was carried from the cross to the sepulcher, and each one of you was asked whether he believed in the name of the Father, and of the Son, and of the Holy Ghost; and ye made that saving confession and descended three times into the water, and ascended again; here also covertly pointing by a figure at the three days' burial of Christ."—(*Lecture* 22.)

BASIL—Born about 326. "This, then, is what is meant by

being borne of water and of the Spirit; death being brought to pass in the water, but life being wrought in us through the Spirit. In three immersions, therefore, and in the same number of invocations, the great mystery of baptism is finished."—(From Modes of Baptism by Chrystal.)

JEROME—Born 331. "We are thrice dipped in water, that the mysteries of the Trinity may appear to be but one; and therefore, though we be thrice put under water, to represent the mystery of the Trinity, yet it is reputed but one baptism." (Translated by Bingham.)

GREGORY NYSSEN—Born about 332. "We who receive baptism in imitation of our Lord and Teacher and Guide, are not buried in the earth, for this covers the entirely lifeless body, and enwraps the weakness and corruption of our natures; but coming to the water, the element cognate to the earth we hide our selves in it, as the Savior hid himself in the earth, and this we do three times, to represent the grace of his resurrection performed after three days."—(On Christ's Baptism.)

AMBROSE—Born 349. "Thou wast asked, 'Dost thou believe in God the Father Almighty?' and thou repliedst, 'I believe,' and was dipped, that is, buried. A second demand was made, 'Dost thou believe in Jesus Christ, our Lord, and in his cross?' thou answereth again, 'I believe,' and wast dipped. Therefore thou wast buried with Christ; for he that is buried with Christ rises again with Christ. A third time the question was repeated, 'Dost thou believe in the Holy Ghost?' and thy answer was, 'I believe,' then thou wast dipped a third time; that the triple confession might absolve thee from the various offences of thy former life." —On the Sacraments.

CHRYSOSTOM—Born 347. "Christ delivered to his disciples one baptism in three immersions of the body, when he said to them. "Go, teach all nations, baptizing them in the name of the Father, and of the Son, and of the Holy Ghost."—(Bingham's Translation.)

PELAGIUS—Born about 350. "There are many who say that they baptize in the name of Christ alone, and by a single immersion. But the Gospel command, which was given by God, himself, and our Lord and Savior, Jesus Christ, reminds us that we should administer holy baptism to every one, in the name of the Trinity and by trine immersion; for our Lord said to his disciples. Go baptize all nations in the name of the Father, and of the Son, and of the Holy Ghost."

APOSTOLIC CONSTITUTIONS—"If any bishop or presbyter does not perform the three immersions of the one admission, but one immersion which is given into the death of Christ, let him be deprived; for the Lord did not say, 'Baptize into my death,' but 'Go ye and make disciples of all nations, baptizing them into the name of the Father, and of the Son, and of the Holy Ghost.' Do ye, therefore, O bishops, baptize thrice into one Father and Son and Holy Ghost, according to the will of Christ and our constitution by the Spirit."—(The oldest collection of Church rules, Canon Fifty, Oxford Translation.)

THEODORET—(Born 393) "He (Eunomius) subverted the holy law of baptism, which had been handed down from the beginning from the Lord and the Apostles, and made a contrary law, asserting that it is not necessary to immerse the candidate for baptism thrice, nor to mention the names of the Trinity, but to immerse once only into the death of Christ."—(From modes of Baptism by Chrystal.)

GELASIUS—(Flourished 490.) "Then let the priest baptize by trine immersion alone, invoking but once the Holy Trinity, and saying thus: And I Baptize thee in the name of the Father, and let him immerse once, and of the Son, and let him immerse a second time, and of the Holy Ghost, and let him immerse a third time."— (*Book of Sacraments*)

GREGORY—(Born about 544.) "The reason we use trine immersion, is to signify the mysteries of Christ's three-day's burial."

HAYMO—(Flourished 850.) "He himself arose on the third day active, and we after a third immersion shall arise to life from the death of sin."

LANFRANCE—(Born 1005.) "For as Christ lay for three days in the sepulcher, so let there be three immersions in baptism."

MARTIN LUTHER—"But as regards the public baptism I am content that covered with a cloth, she shall sit in a tub, with the water reaching to the neck, clad with the bathing-cloth, and that she shall be three times dipped with the head into the water by the baptizer with the usual words—namely, 'I baptize you into the name of the Father, and of the Son, and of the Holy

Ghost, Amen."—(*Directions to a Minister* regarding the Baptism of a Jewish Lady. Translated from the German.)

DUPIN—"Baptism was administered to infants and adults. They were dipped three times into the water."—(Remarks on the *Discipline of the Church* in the Fourth Century.)

WALL—"The way of Trine Immersion, or plunging the head of the person three times into the water, was the general practice of all antiquity.—(*Infant Baptism*, Vol. 2, Page 419.)

BEVERIDGE—"Neither did the Church ever esteem that Baptism valid which was not administered exactly according to the institution in the name of all the Three Persons; which the primitive Christians were so strict in the observance of, that it was enjoined that all persons to be baptized should be plunged three times into the water, first at the 'Name of the Father,' and then at the 'Name of the Son.' and lastly at the 'Name of the Holy Ghost."—(*Works*, Vol. 8, page 336.)

DAILLE—"I confess that that custom of thrice immersing the person to be baptized is most ancient among Christians."— (Quoted by Bishop Beveridge.)

Dr. Armitage, author of a very complete Baptist history says in describing the traditional spot of the immersion of Jesus "Its thick mellow groves are used as robing rooms, whence Copts and Syrians, Armenians and Greeks, go down into the Jordan and immerse themselves three times in the name of the Trinity." (Page 29.)

Dean Stanley says: "On philological grounds it is quite correct to translate John the Baptist by John the Immerser." (Armitage's *Baptist History*, page 30.)

ONE LINE OF SUCCESSION

James Chrystal published in 1861 *A History of the Modes of Baptism*, a very dependable volume of over 300 pages in close print on Baptism. He was a minister in the Protestant Episcopal Church and long a teacher of Greek.

Here is a copy of part of his written statement concerning his own Baptism and the writer's.

This is to certify that Aaron L. Garber, now of Ashland, Ohio, came to me for the ancient successional trine immersion.

This Lord's Day, Aug. 22, P.M. 1880, I baptized in the Baptismal pool of the North Baptist Church, Jersey City, N. J., Aaron L. Garber. I dipped him totally thrice, and the baptism was perfect.

The undersigned was himself baptized by the three total immersions. On the eve of Epiphany, January 6, 1869, at Syra in Greece, by Alexander Lycurgus, the Greek Archbishop of that See.   James Chrystal."

This is one more testimony, and a strong one that the three dip immersion, came down from the beginning of the Christian Church in a direct successional line.

TRINE IMMERSION BAPTISM

Every reliable Church historian and theological writer, ancient and modern, who had occasion to discourse upon the modes of baptism, admits that Trine Immersion was the general practice of the Primitive Church in all parts of the world, and that it continued to be until far into the dark ages. The authors quoted above rank with the brightest names on the monument of Christian Literature, and many of them knew no superior in learning and ability in their respective ages. Tertullian, the first of the great Latin Fathers of the Church was born almost at the foot of the Apostolic age, when those were yet living who saw and heard the last one of the twelve, who transmitted the saving revelation to the keeping of faithful shepherds, that enriched the earth by giving their bodies to be consumed to ashes, and attested their faith in torrents of blood; and he, with his keenness of discernment, the resources of a liberal and comprehensive education, an extensive acquaintance with the institutions and doctrines of his day, the privileges of a Latin scholar of enviable reputation, a wide association with men of learning in the Church, and with great zeal for the cause, could not have failed to know the character and practice of the first and great Ordinance in the Faith which he held and so ably defended, in his day, the doctrine of the Trinity held by the Universal Church was assailed, and in his arguments in its support he brings forward the three manifestations in the act of baptism, at the naming of the Three Persons of the Trinity. From this time the mode of baptism was not a question of controversy, unless regarding the validity of the irregular baptism of sick-beds, until a single immersion was set up and performed into the death of Christ by Eunomius. The law of baptism was assailed thereby, and the writings which have come down to us are full of proofs of Trine Immersion, as the above quotations show, which are only a few of the many, and the Church rubrics bear testimony to the fact, by forbidding baptism to be performed into the death of Christ, instead of using the scriptural formula. It seems also that an irregular use of the names of the Trinity arose at this time, which caused them to be very precise in defining the proper mode. At the close of this period the dark ages came on, and the Latin and Greek branches of the Church broke off all communication with one another. The former developed into the great Anti-Christ, while the victorious Mohammedan armies settled over the latter as a wilderness. The Roman Communion abandoned the primitive baptism and used affusion, but the Eastern continued the three dip Immersion and practice it at the present time, to the exclusion of all other modes.

That Three dip Immersion was the general practice of all antiquity, and was received from the Apostles, no man with any reputation as a scholar will undertake to deny.

Trine Immersion was the general practice of all Chistendom for the first ten centuries of the Christian Era.

Trine Immersion is the Baptism the Greek Church received from the Apostles and carefully maintained through all the subsequent ages, and practice it today.

Trine Immersion is the only mode approved received as valid Baptism by the three great stems of the Church, today, the Greek, Latin and the Anglican.

Trine Immersion was the general practice of the Church of England up to the commencement of the sixteenth century.

Trine Immersion is the Baptism taught and enjoined by all the Church offices, rubrics, rituals and councils, of any importance and authority, for twelve hundred years after Christ.

Trine Immersion is the Baptism of more than two hundred millions of professing Christians.

Trine Immersion is The True Baptism.

ADMINISTERING BAPTISM

The ritual of Baptism was divinely given by the resurrected Jesus, in these words, Baptizing them in the name of the Father and in the name of the Son and in the name of the Holy Spirit. It is of interest to discern that the Son is the Reborn Son, the Jesus of the resurrection who is living Christ.

In the three dip immersion baptism, the large part of the body is immersed only once. The head of the candidate rises out of the water only, first in introduction to the Father, dips again and rises in introduction to the Son, dips again and the body rises in introduction to the Holy Spirit, to walk in newness of life. Thus the three are acknowledged.

The method of performing three dip immersion generally is called Trine Immersion.

There is no forward or backward plunging in the primitive mode of Baptism, which was distinctly a believer's Baptism.

The Baptizer leads the applicant into the water until it comes up in the arm pits to the arms. He directs the applicant to put his hands on his legs just above his knees, or with his arms straight down and hands on his legs. The baptizer puts one hand on the applicants head and the other grasping his shoulder. Then as he speaks the ritual he presses down on the candidate and he drops straight down on one knee—a kneeling on one knee only. He gently bows his head forward in place of being thrown into the water. Then with his hands above his knees he helps himself to rise to his feet for the second dip, then on to the third dip. This way is suitable where there is much water. Gospel Baptism does not assume that the administrator must be a person of great physical strength. His chief service is to use the ritual as a servant of Christ, and with strong applicants all that is necessary is to press down on his head, as he speaks the name and the applicant sinks himself in the water and rises to complete the acts. In this primitive method the applicant is not at any time put in an attitude of physical dependence in the hands of the baptizer.

There is no need to be technical about the manner of dipping in Baptism. The conditions are so different in the depth of the water that the administrator must decide on the standing or kneeling posture and the sinking or plunging forward in the act. St. Paul speaks plainly on this point in *Rom.* 6:3-5. Baptism into Jesus Christ is baptism into his death, and a burial with him, and it is in the likeness of his death.

The history of the death of Jesus is, that he bowed his head and died. John 19:30.

It is not in the likeness of his burial, yet it is a burial.

The three dip immersion in the succession is as a title deed to historical Christianity.

The Single Immersion Baptism now common was introduced by John Smith of England, who with others gathered in Holland. To begin an assembly, he baptized himself, in a single immersion, then the others of the company.

Roger Williams began the Baptist Church of America in 1639. Ezekiel Holliman baptized Roger Williams and he then baptized Mr. Holliman and ten others.

The Tunker Baptism now common in the United States is not linked in with the three dip baptism of the succession. It was adopted by reformers of the Presbyterian faith in 1708 in France. Lots were cast on who should begin the mode, and the one chosen was kept secret. He baptized the leader, Alexander Mack. He then baptized his administrator and the others of a company of eight.

The statement has already been made that this writing is not to be a judge. What is past is a matter with the individual and the Lord. The right to teach remains and there is no reason that can forbid the presentation of the truth on which is the mode that was introduced in the founding of the Christian Church, as a token for the forgiveness of sins. After this, the individual can use his own volition.

Many synods, councils in the record of history support the trine immersion along with many other authorities which are not taken up in this appendix. The evidence herein is sufficient for the neutral investigator.

It is a grief to observe how some teachers mislead themselves and others into the belief that Apostolic Baptism was a single immersion and only in the name of Jesus Christ. *Act.* 2:38 is used to establish the claim. Strange it is that the exhortation is made to deny the commission of Jesus Christ, risen from the dead, given to the Apostles, and to all, the three dip immersion which was planted in every Apostolic church, proven by subsequent history—the three dips in one immersion, as the larger part of the body remains in the water until the three dips are performed.

There are those who have been baptized in one of the compend modes that will be anxious about being baptized in the regular mode. Let all such know that there can be no sin, no wrong, in being baptized again.

Baptism in the name of Jesus Christ means, under his authority, according to his teaching, in harmony with his command, but not a ceremony of mode.

The changes in the mode came in the human disposition of men to drift away from the institutions the Lord gave; and others, no doubt, in ignorance of the history of the past. In the countries where papal dominion pulled the curtain of ignorance over the people, it would have been only human to suppose that there was no other practice than the one they grew up in.

The spirit of reformation was sent upon the people by the Lord and the breaking away from the decretals of the Roman rule by Luther and others stirred up the spirit of reformation in many. Even John Smith who began the single immersion by the baptizing of himself to make a beginning, left England, his home country, and went to Holland to gain freedom of action and escape possible death.

The candor of the statements presented herein is evidence that the purpose is not the defence of the practice of some denomination but to support the mode of Primitive Christianity which has come down the ages to the present.

There is no way that satisfies the heart like doing what has the surest claim of being right before the Lord.

MY CONVERSION

As a converted Roman Catholic, I was trained in the monasteries to observe diligently the ordinances of the Roman Catholic Church, which I supposed to be the true church of Christ. In the course of time, however, I noticed that its professions do not tally with its practices. Moreover, I discovered that it is not in accord with the Holy Scriptures, and therefore I renounced it. But I could find no peace of mind with the Protestants, either. At last a copy of the Papal Primacy and certain other works of Apostolos Makrakis fell into my hands. A perusal of his Philosophical System, Catechism, and the Memoir concerning the nature of the Christian Church convinced me that he was a true teacher of Christianity with a divine mission. He unfolded the doctrine of Christ's church, which is the One Holy Catholic Apostolic (Greek Orthodox) Church, The Roman Catholic Church is inimical and opposed to Christ's Church. The Greek Orthodox Church is that which was established by the Apostles and the Holy Fathers, i.e., the Seven Ecumenical Councils. Union of all churches with the Orthodox Church will bring about the defeat of the enemy Satan and of all his institutions, but, of course, all the churches must first unite themselves with Christ and His laws; then they will **ipso facto** become united with the Orthodox Christians. The Orthodox Church is not seeking to rule over the Catholics and Protestants; what it wants is cooperation as one church of Christ, with the same dogma and canons. Christ's Church is distinguished by adhering to the dogma and the canonical laws of the Apostles and the Ecumenical Councils. A church of Christ cannot function without a dogma and canonical laws derived from Christ and the Holy Spirit, just as no nation or political state can function without a constitution and statutes. The dogma and canons set forth by the Holy Fathers constitute in fact the Church. The original church was founded by Christ and the Holy Spirit (the two true witnesses of God) through the Apostles and the Seven Ecumenical Councils. Christ's Church, dogma and canons are one thing, and the clergy and laity another—just as a political state and its constitution and statutes are one thing, and the rulers and people another. Christ and the Holy Spirit founded only one church. Men founded the many churches. This is the Orthodox view.

By studying the works of the great teacher of Christianity Apostolos Makrakis, I have found Christ to be the truth, and in uniting through right belief with Him I have by the same token united myself with His One Holy Catholic Apostolic Orthodox Church. Apostolos Makrakis was indeed the true Messenger of Christ and herald of mankind's salvation. I recommend that everyone study the books of Makrakis and learn the truth, for the truth will set them free from the errors that beset both Romanism and Protestantism.

Basil Quinn.

TITLES BY APOSTOLOS MAKRAKIS

A New Original Philosophical System (2 vols.) ....per set *$15.00
The Foundation of Philosophy 4.00
The Bible and the World, and Triluminal Science (1 vol.) 5.00
Interpretation of the Entire New Testament
   (except the Book of Revelation) — (2 vols.) .... per set 20.00
An Interpretation of the Gospel Law 5.00
An Interpretation of the Book of Revelation 5.00
The Paramount Doctrine of Orthodoxy (3 books in one volume)..... 8.00
Commentary of the Psalms of David and the Nine Odes............ 10.00
Concerning Our Duties to God 2.00
Kryiakodromion, or Sunday Sermonary, and Festal Sermons........ 6.00
I. Three Great Friday Sermons; II. Three Sermons of The Death on the
   Cross and the Glorius Resurrection; III. The Ascension into Heaven;
   IV. Christ, Announcing His Nature; V. All the Parables of the Gospels;
   VI. The Truth in Christianity; VII. Testimonies Concerning the Super
   Holy Virgin. All in One Volume.
Freemasonry Known by Masonic Diploma 2.00
Divine and Sacred Catechism 3.00
Papal Primacy and Innovations of Roman Catholic Church 1.00
Scriptural Refutations of Pope's Primacy, and Misc. 1.00
Memoir on the Nature of the Church of Christ 2.50
The Two Contrariant Schools, and Concerning the Establishment of
   a Christian University (1 vol. paper bound) 1.00
An Orthodox-Protestant Debate 1.00
A Revelation of Treasure Hid 1.00
Proofs of the Authenticity of the Septuagint .... .50
God's Law and Commandments, the Decalogue and the Gospel...... 1.00
The Repose of Our Most Holy and Glorious Lady The Theotocos..... 50
The City of Zion, or The Church Built Upon the Rock 2.00
Philosophical Discussions .... .50
The Real Truth Concerning Apostolos Makrakis 2.00
The RUDDER OR PEDALION, of the Metaphorical Ship of the Holy
   Catholic and Apostolic Church of Orthodox Christians
   (All the Sacred and Divine Canons) 10.00
The Trial of Jesus Christ (by Abba Aristarchus) 1.00

---

*NOTE: All prices given herein are quoted U.S. Funds.

5043-4
306

Publishers and Advocates of Orthodox Christian Literature

THE ORTHODOX CHRISTIAN EDUCATIONAL SOCIETY

1956 Henderson Street   **231 - 3rd Street**
Chicago, Ill. 60657   **New Westminster, B. C. Canada**